The Paleo Diet Cookbook

More Than 150 Recipes for Paleo Breakfasts, Lunches, Dinners, Snacks, and Beverages

Loren Cordain, Ph.D.

with Nell Stephenson and Lorrie Cordain

WILEY

John Wiley & Sons, Inc.

ISBN 978-0-470-91304-8 (paper); ISBN 978-1-118-01270-3 (ebk); ISBN 978-1-118-01271-0 (ebk); ISBN 978-1-118-01272-7 (ebk)

Printed in the United States of America

10

For Marji and Dick
—Loren Cordain

For Pat and Dennis
—Lorrie Cordain

To my husband, Chris, and my mom, Ellen
—Nell Stephenson

CONTENTS

ACKNOWLEDGMENTS

Writing a book is always a labor of love, involving countless hours and the generosity of numerous people with their time, dedication, and hard work. However, this book would never have come about were it not for you, my faithful readers and followers of the Paleo Diet, who have popularized humanity's ancestral diet and made "Paleo" a household word—thank you!

I want to especially express gratitude to my agent, Channa Taub, who tirelessly worked with us to create a book from simply an idea. Her warm enthusiasm and steady guidance over seemingly endless hours on the telephone are truly appreciated and made the arduous task of writing seem almost fun. Thanks to Tom Miller, my editor, for his enduring support and commitment to the Paleo Diet concept since its inception. Appreciation is due to Nell Stephenson for her passion and loyalty to the Paleo way of eating.

A special apology goes out to "the boys" for the summer that wasn't—someday you will understand. And finally, thanks to Lorrie for her unwavering support and love over the past twenty years. I have enjoyed the ride.

—LOREN CORDAIN

Twenty-one years ago, on the shores of beautiful Lake Tahoe, I attended the wedding of a friend and was introduced to Dr. Loren Cordain. Little did I know at the time that I was about to embark on a journey with an individual who would change the way millions of people view diet, nutrition, and the concept of healthy living. It has been my good fortune to participate in the quiet revolution that began with a simple question: what is the optimal human diet, and how does it relate to overall health?

Through dedication, perseverance, and integrity, Loren has answered this question and has systematically outlined for the scientific world, as well as the layperson, the link between the human diet and overall well-being. Together we have embraced the concept of the Paleo Diet, and we faithfully live by its principles. Most gratifying have been the countless testimonials from people all over the world who have written that after adopting the diet, they have rid themselves of lifelong ailments, eliminated the chronic symptoms of modern disease, and discovered renewed energy and vibrant health.

I want to thank Loren for his hard work, his commitment to answering the fundamental questions, and his unselfishness in mentoring countless individuals in successfully eliminating their health problems and restoring their vitality. Thank you, Loren. I too have enjoyed the ride.

In addition, I would like to thank my parents for the sacrifices they have made to help me reach my dreams. I am forever grateful. To my brother, Michael, my sincerest gratitude for your years of love and support during our incredible adventures together. You have enriched my life. I must express my appreciation to my three sons, Kyle, Kevin, and Kenny, for all of their patience and understanding when their parents were working nonstop to meet deadlines.

Thank you to Nell Stephenson for her contributions and her enthusiasm for this book. Special thanks to Channa Taub for her advice and her confidence in my writing abilities. Finally, thanks to Tom Miller for his willingness to take on this project and see it through to fruition.

—LORRIE CORDAIN

Growing up with a hippie mom was my introduction to a healthy approach to eating and being active, so much so that it's always been an intrinsic part of who I am. Although at the time I was always the odd kid out, with raw veggies and cashews in my lunch while all the other children ate bologna on white bread, I now have nothing but appreciation for my mom's dedication to making sure I ate only real food. Thank you for that, Mom!

I must acknowledge my wonderful husband, training partner, and best friend, Chris, for always encouraging and motivating me to follow my passion in nutrition and fitness and turn it into a successful business, and for being my number one taste tester for years' worth of countless dishes, meals, and elaborate dinner parties that I've created or reinvented as Paleo-friendly foods.

Finally, thanks to Loren, not only for inviting me to coauthor this book but also for the decades of research that have gone into the Paleo Diet, which I truly believe is the way that all human beings were meant to eat. It has so significantly changed my life, my athletic performance, and my nutritional counseling business practices that I cannot imagine where I'd be if I had never discovered it. It's been a wonderful opportunity to have worked with him and Lorrie, whose experience and expertise have been invaluable and with whom I've enjoyed collaborating tremendously.

—NELL STEPHENSON

Introduction

The Paleo Diet Cookbook represents a practical plan for you and your family to cook and eat the healthiest diet on the planet—the diet to help you optimize your health and normalize your weight. The benefits of this lifetime way of eating are enormous: You will have more energy throughout the day. You will sleep better. Your mental outlook will improve, and all indices of your health and well-being will soar.

The diet is incredibly easy to follow—eat fresh fruits, fresh veggies, lean meats, and seafood. Stick to the outside aisles of your supermarket and away from the center aisles, and you will be 85 percent of the way there. As you increasingly shun foods made with refined sugars, grains, vegetable oils, and salt, your palate will respond positively to the incredible cornucopia of flavors and textures and wealth of tastes that reside in real foods. Highly salted, sweetened, and processed foods blunt our palates to the subtle flavors of nature's real groceries. With the Paleo Diet, a fresh strawberry becomes exquisitely sweet and just right, whereas a fancy chocolate becomes too sweet—an artificial adulteration of the real thing that sends your blood sugar rushing up and then down, making you feel bad in the end.

Sometimes it's not so much what you eat but what you don't eat that affects your health and well-being. Scientific evidence increasingly implicates grains, dairy products, legumes, and processed foods in metabolic syndrome diseases (type 2 diabetes, heart disease, high blood pressure, gout, acne, and more), cancer, autoimmune diseases, and others. In fact, I know of very few chronic illnesses that don't respond positively to the Paleo Diet.

If you have these diseases or just want to lose a little weight and improve your overall health, what better way to do so than by enjoying the Paleo cuisine we offer you in *The Paleo Diet Cookbook*? With its more than 150 recipes, two-week meal plan, and hundreds of helpful hints for preparing, cooking, and serving Paleo foods, you will become a winner (and also a loser, if you need to drop some weight).

With *The Paleo Diet Cookbook*, I'm pleased to introduce you to my team of culinary experts, whose decades of combined experience with humanity's original diet will make this way of eating and preparing food simple, appetizing, and second nature to you. My wife and lifelong companion, Lorrie, has probably been eating Paleo style longer than anyone on the planet, except for the few remaining hunter-gatherers. Lorrie has been preparing innovative and delicious Paleo meals and snacks for nearly twenty years. She single-handedly produced nearly every recipe in my first book, *The Paleo Diet*.

Lorrie's interests run far and wide; she is not only an accomplished Paleo chef, a former triathlete, marathon runner, and high school cross-country coach, and a wonderful mother and wife, but she is also an experienced teacher with master's degrees in both elementary and special education. Lorrie has a special talent for merging my scientific writings with many of Nell Stephenson's innovative recipes to produce a book that is lively, coherent, and relevant to today's cuisine.

Nell Stephenson is an internationally recognized Ironman triathlete, marathon runner, personal fitness consultant, and nutritional counselor, and like Lorrie she is also a Paleo chef. In her personal quest, Nell experimented with nearly every nutritional plan under the sun. She eventually discovered the Paleo Diet and found it to be superior to all other ways of eating. Nell has become a staunch supporter of the Paleo Diet and has years of practical experience in prescribing this lifetime plan of eating to her international clientele, including athletes as well as people just trying to lose weight and regain their health.

With a bachelor's degree in exercise science from the University of Southern California, culinary school experience, and more than a decade of wisdom garnered in the fitness and nutrition industry, Nell brings important practical experience to the recipes that she and Lorrie have created for this book. Based in Los Angeles, she can be contacted through her Web site, www.nellstephenson.com.

The Paleo Diet Cookbook owes its origin to the resounding international popularity of my first book, *The Paleo Diet*. Although it was published several years ago, it has steadily sold more and more copies over the ensuing years and has recently risen into the top ten best-selling diet and health books. Such a sales history for a diet or health book is almost unheard of, as books of this genre typically sell like hotcakes when first released but then rapidly fade into oblivion. I have now thoroughly revised and updated *The Paleo Diet*; *The Paleo Diet, Revised Edition*, which has just been published, reflects the latest scientific research and revisions to the diet, as does this cookbook.

The Paleo Diet and *The Paleo Diet Cookbook* are different from all other diet books and cookbooks in that they outline a lifetime program of eating based not upon the fallible ideas of charismatic diet doctors whose books eventually wither away, but rather upon our species' ancestral diet. This is the foundational diet to which we are all genetically adapted and the diet consumed by every single human being on the planet a mere 333 generations ago.

When we restore our diet to the one for which we are genetically adapted, chronic illnesses and diseases with obscure or currently unknown causes improve or completely disappear. For instance, dermatologists once told us that diet had little or nothing to do with acne. Fast-forward to 2010, and the best medical and nutritional journals in the world now recognize that the typical Western diet—filled with processed foods, sugars, dairy products, and cereal grains—represents the main trigger of this common skin disease. Research from my scientific group in 2002 broke the diet-acne story wide open with our publication in the flagship dermatology journal, *Archives of Dermatology*.

My insight for uncovering acne's dietary basis came from the evolutionary template that is the foundation for the Paleo Diet as well as for the delicious foods you will soon be preparing from the recipes and meal plans in *The Paleo Diet Cookbook*. This organizational template has allowed me and other scientists worldwide to uncover the optimal human diet. This nutritional scheme was not only the dietary master plan for our hunter-gatherer ancestors, but remains so for all of us today.

The Paleo Diet and even the word "Paleo" itself have become household concepts in the past decade, with recent coverage in the *New York Times*, the *Washington Post*, and other national and international media. A few years ago, if you searched for "Paleo Diet" with an Internet search engine, you would have been lucky to find my Web site, www.thepaleodiet.com. Now the Internet is literally bursting with Web sites, people, products, and services catering to this concept.

The world has rapidly embraced this concept because it works. If you are overweight, the Paleo Diet will help you to lose weight effortlessly and without constant hunger. If you have high blood pressure, high cholesterol, type 2 diabetes, or cardiovascular disease, the Paleo Diet will swiftly improve your disease symptoms. In the past decade, thousands of scientific studies have verified the nutritional concepts I originally laid out in my first book.

In *The Paleo Diet Cookbook*, you will discover an incredible wealth of scrumptious, mouthwatering foods that will restore your vigor and guarantee your birthright of a long and healthy life.

The Paleo Diet
Basics

Many of you have read my first book, *The Paleo Diet*, and are longtime Paleo Dieters with years of experience under your belts. For both you and for newcomers to the concept, *The Paleo Diet Cookbook* will provide a wealth of new Paleo recipes and menu plans that we have created, along with hundreds of helpful food, preparation, and cooking tips.

In this chapter, for the benefit of Paleo newbies as well as veterans, I will review the basics of the Paleo Diet, since a number of key points have changed since the first book's publication in 2002. *The Paleo Diet, Revised Edition*, which has just been published, contains the latest essential updates to the plan.

The Paleo Diet: A Simple
Nutritional Formula

The diet that nature intended for us is simplicity itself. You don't have to count calories, keep dietary logs, or even measure portions. Instead, the essential rules of the Paleo Diet are incredibly easy: all the lean meats, poultry, fish, seafood, fruits (except dried fruits), and vegetables (except potatoes and corn) you can consume. Since the foundation of the Paleo Diet is high-quality, low-fat protein foods, don't feel guilty about eating lean meat, poultry, fish, or seafood at every meal—it is precisely what you need to do, along with adding as many fresh fruits and vegetables as you like.

When you follow the uncomplicated nutritional principles laid out in this chapter and later spelled out in the book's delicious, easy recipes and meal plans, you will lose weight, reduce your risk of metabolic syndrome (high blood pressure, heart disease, and type 2 diabetes), cancer, autoimmune diseases, and virtually every other chronic illness that afflicts modern societies. You will sleep better, you will have increased libido, and you will have an even energy level throughout the day. Best of all, you won't feel hungry all day long on this diet, because its high protein content is the best satisfier of the brain's appetite center. If you eat a high-protein lunch, you will eat fewer calories not only at this meal but also at dinner.

By mimicking the diets of our hunter-gatherer ancestors with common everyday foods that you can purchase at your local supermarket or grow in your own backyard, you'll be able to reap the health benefits that are your birthright: freedom from obesity, vigor, and optimal health throughout your life span. It is not crucial to exactly duplicate hunter-gatherer diets. This would be a next-to-impossible task in our twenty-first-century world, as many of those foods are no longer in existence, are commercially unavailable, or are simply unpalatable to our contemporary tastes and cultural biases.

For instance, hunter-gatherers typically ate the entire animal—brains, eyeballs, tongue, marrow, liver, kidneys, intestines, gonads—whereas these organs are unappetizing to most of us. However, these differences need not present any nutritional shortcomings in modern-day versions of our ancestral diet, particularly if we include seafood, fish, healthy oils, and a wide variety of fruits and veggies.

The Three Levels of the Paleo Diet and the 85-15 Rule

Most adults in the United States and other Westernized countries have never gone through a single day in their lives without eating grains, dairy products, refined sugars, or processed food. So, believe me, I have compassion for you when I ask you to forgo certain foods that have probably been daily staples for most of your life. It clearly isn't easy to alter the habits of a lifetime, but you don't have to do it all at once. You can soften the transition by easing into the Paleo Diet progressively, in a series of three levels of adherence. The levels are designed with the idea that what you do occasionally won't sidetrack the healthy benefits of what you do most of the time.

Does this mean you can occasionally cheat? Absolutely. The flexibility of the Paleo Diet allows you to cheat occasionally, without losing the diet's overall health benefits. Infrequent cheating is a great psychological strategy to help you adhere to the diet most of the time, and it won't necessarily derail the weight loss and health effects you are trying to achieve. The only exceptions are for people with severe illnesses or autoimmune diseases, who should try for 100 percent compliance. Keep in mind that many people find that once they abandon a favorite food, its reintroduction makes them feel so awful that they simply have little or no desire to eat it again.

The key to the three compliance levels of *The Paleo Diet* is what I call the 85-15 rule. Most people eat about twenty meals a week, plus snacks. Consequently, three meals per week represent 15 percent of your weekly meals. At Level 1 of the Paleo Diet, you can cheat 15 percent of the time by including three Open Meals per week. At Level 2, you are allowed to cheat 10 percent of the time, with two Open Meals per week, and finally at Level 3 you are permitted a single Open Meal, which represents 5 percent of your total weekly meals. The beauty of this tactic is that you don't have to forgo your favorite foods completely and forever. I recommend that beginners start at Level 1 for a few weeks and then gradually move toward Level 3 as they become accustomed to the diet.

What to Eat, What to Avoid

For Paleo Diet novices, one of the key issues that frequently arises is the proper amount of plant and animal foods that should be eaten on a regular basis. The best way to answer this question is to follow the example of our hunter-gatherer ancestors. My research demonstrates that although there was no single Stone Age diet, animal food was always favored over plant food. Our analysis of 229 hunter-gatherer societies showed that animal foods composed about 60 percent of the total daily caloric intake. On the Paleo Diet, you should therefore try to obtain a little more than half of your calories from lean meat, organ meats, poultry, seafood, and fish. The remainder should come from plant foods. A general rule of thumb is to put a fist-sized piece of meat or fish on your plate and then fill the remainder of your plate with fruits and veggies.

Although you will entirely eliminate three food groups (grains, dairy, and legumes) along with processed foods, you will be amazed at the astonishing diversity of healthy and delicious foods that you may never have considered. Let's examine these incredibly varied foods.

Animal Foods

One of the essential concepts of the Paleo Diet is to eat animal food at nearly every meal. But the key idea here is one of quality and freshness. Always try to eat your meat, fish, poultry, and seafood as fresh as possible. Fresh is almost always best, followed by frozen; stay away from canned, tinned, processed, smoked, or salted animal foods. When it comes to beef, pork, and chicken, free-ranging, grass-fed, or pasture-produced meats are best, albeit a bit pricey. Try your local farmers' market or go to my friend Jo Robinson's Web site, www.eatwild.com/ to find a farmer or a rancher in your vicinity who can supply you with unadulterated, grass-produced meats.

Feedlot and Grain-Produced Meats

Ninety-nine percent of the beef, pork, and chicken produced in the United States comes from enormous feedlots, which sometimes contain up to a hundred thousand animals. The driving force behind feedlot-produced meat is almost purely economic. The objective of these huge corporate agribusinesses is to turn out the largest, heaviest animals possible as rapidly as possible with the least amount of feed. To accomplish this goal, the animals are confined in small spaces, where they get little exercise and are fed unlimited amounts of grain. Does this situation sound familiar?

The end result is not pretty. Feedlot-produced cattle maintain a four- to six-inch layer of white fat covering their entire body. These artificial products of modern agriculture are overweight and sick. Their muscles are frequently infiltrated with fat, which we call marbling, a trait that improves flavor but makes the cattle insulin-resistant and unhealthy, just like humans. Because feedlot-raised animals are exclusively fed grains (corn and sorghum) in the last half of their lives, their meat is concentrated with omega 6 fatty acids at the expense of health-promoting omega 3 fatty acids.

The bottom line is that the nutritional characteristics of feed-lot-produced meat are generally inferior to those of meat from grass-fed or free-ranging animals. However, as was the case in my first book, I still believe that some, but not all, of these meats can be a healthy part of the Paleo Diet, particularly if you try to obtain the leaner cuts and eat fatty fish like salmon a few times a week. The table below shows the differences in total fat and protein content between lean and fatty cuts of meat.

What's Wrong with Processed Meats?

In the first edition of *The Paleo Diet*, I was steadfast in my advice that you should steer clear of fatty processed meats like bologna,

FAT AND PROTEIN CONTENT (Percentage of Total Calories in Lean and Fatty Meats)					
Meats You Should Eat	% Protein	% Fat	Meats You Should Avoid	% Protein	% Fat
Skinless turkey breast	94	5	T-bone steak	36	64
Buffalo roast	84	16	Chicken thigh/leg	36	63
Roast venison	81	19	Ground beef (15% fat)	35	63
Pork tenderloin, lean	72	28	Lamb shoulder roast	32	68
Beef heart	69	30	Pork ribs	27	73
Veal steak	68	32	Beef ribs	26	74
Sirloin beef steak	65	35	Fatty lamb chop	25	75
Chicken liver	65	32	Dry salami	23	75
Skinless chicken breast	63	37	Pork link sausage	22	77
Beef liver	63	28	Bacon	21	78
Lean beef flank steak	62	38	Bologna	15	81
Lean pork chop	62	38	Hot dog	14	83

bacon, hot dogs, lunch meat, salami, and sausage. That message still holds true, and you can see from the table that processed meats are more like fat disguised as meat. Processed meats are synthetic mixtures of meat and fat; they are artificially combined at the meatpacker or butcher's whim with no consideration for the actual fatty acid profile of the wild animals our Stone Age ancestors ate. Besides their unnatural fatty acid compositions (high in omega 6 fatty acids, low in omega 3 fatty acids, and high in saturated fatty acids), fatty processed meats contain preservatives called nitrites and nitrates, which are converted into powerful cancer-causing nitrosamines in our gut. Furthermore, these unnatural meats are typically laced with salt, high-fructose corn syrup, grains, and other additives that have many undesirable health effects.

With the Paleo Diet I encourage you to eat as much high-quality real animal foods that you can get your hands on. Obviously, the closer you can get to wild, the better off you'll be when it comes to the fatty acid profile and the nutrient content of your meat. Game meat is not necessary for the Paleo Diet, but if you want to be adventuresome, try some. It's nutritious and adds a unique flavor and twist to any Paleo meal. Game meat is pricey (unless you hunt or know hunters), and typically only available at specialty markets, farmers' markets, and certain butcher stores.

Use the following list to help you select healthy meats for the delicious recipes in the chapters that follow.

LEAN MEATS

LEAN BEEF

- Flank steak
- Top sirloin steak
- Extra-lean hamburger (extra fat drained off)
- London broil
- Chuck steak
- Lean veal
- Any other lean cut

LEAN LAMB

- Grass-fed lamb chops from Australia or New Zealand
- Grass-fed lamb roasts from Australia or New Zealand

LEAN PORK

- Pork loin
- Pork chops
- Any other lean cut

LEAN POULTRY (white meat, skin removed)

- Chicken breast
- Turkey breast
- Game hen breast

OTHER MEATS

- Rabbit meat (any cut)
- Goat meat (any cut)
- Escargot

ORGAN MEATS

- Beef, lamb, pork, and chicken liver
- Beef, pork, and lamb tongue
- Beef, lamb, and pork marrow
- Beef, lamb, and pork sweetbreads

GAME MEAT

- Alligator or crocodile
- Bear
- Bison or buffalo
- Caribou
- Elk
- Emu
- Frog legs
- Goose
- Kangaroo
- Muscovy duck
- New Zealand Cervena deer
- Ostrich
- Pheasant
- Quail
- Rattlesnake
- Reindeer
- Squab
- Squirrel
- Turtle
- Venison
- Wild boar
- Wild turkey

Fish, Seafood, and Shellfish

Fish, seafood, and shellfish are some of the healthiest animal foods you can eat, and they are a cornerstone of the Paleo Diet because they are rich sources of the healthy long-chain omega 3 fatty acids known as EPA and DHA. Fatty fish, such as salmon, mackerel, and herring, are particularly rich in both of these long-chain omega 3 fatty acids. Try to include fish in your menu at least three times a week. Here's a list of fish and shellfish that are key players in any modern-day version of the Paleo Diet.

FISH

- Bass
- Bluefish
- Cod
- Drum
- Eel
- Flatfish
- Grouper
- Haddock
- Halibut
- Herring
- Mackerel
- Monkfish
- Mullet
- Northern pike
- Orange roughy
- Perch
- Red snapper
- Rockfish
- Salmon
- Scrod
- Shark
- Striped bass
- Sunfish
- Tilapia
- Trout
- Tuna
- Turbot
- Walleye
- Any commercially available fish

SHELLFISH

- Abalone
- Calamari (squid)
- Crab
- Crayfish
- Lobster
- Mussels
- Octopus
- Oysters
- Scallops
- Shrimp

In addition to being an excellent source of EPA and DHA, fish and seafood represent one of our best high-protein foods. The high protein content of the Paleo Diet is central to many of its weight-loss benefits. Protein helps you to lose weight more rapidly by raising your metabolism while simultaneously curbing your hunger. Additionally, protein lowers your total blood cholesterol concentrations as it simultaneously increases the good HDL molecules that rid your body of excessive cholesterol. Finally, protein stabilizes blood sugar and reduces the risk of high blood pressure, stroke, heart disease, and certain cancers.

What about Eggs?

Although eggs are a relatively high-fat food (62 percent fat, 34 percent protein) and are one of the most concentrated sources of dietary cholesterol (212 milligrams per egg), almost all recent scientific studies have concluded that regular egg consumption (seven per week) does not increase the risk for heart disease. You can now find eggs at your local supermarket that are enriched with the healthy long-chain omega 3 fatty acids, EPA and DHA. So go ahead and enjoy this highly nutritious food; just don't overdo it.

Fruits and Vegetables

The ground rules for fruits and veggies on the Paleo Diet are pretty simple. If you are lean and healthy, eat as much of these nutritious foods as you like, but make sure they are as fresh as you can get them. The only banned vegetables are potatoes and corn. Potatoes are excluded because they maintain high glycemic loads that may adversely affect your blood sugar and insulin levels. Corn actually is not a vegetable, but rather is a grain, and like all other grains was not a staple component of preagricultural diets.

Fruits are Mother Nature's natural sweets, and the only fruits you should completely avoid are canned fruits packed in syrup. Dried fruits should be consumed in limited quantities, as they can contain as much concentrated sugar as a candy bar (see the table below). If you are obese or have one or more diseases of metabolic syndrome (hypertension, type 2 diabetes, heart disease, or abnormal blood lipids), you should avoid dried fruit altogether and eat sparingly the very high and high sugar fresh fruits that are listed below. Once your weight normalizes and your disease symptoms wane, feel free to eat as much fresh fruit as you like.

SUGAR CONTENT IN DRIED AND FRESH FRUITS

DRIED FRUITS

Extremely High in Total Sugars	Total Sugars per 100 Grams
Dried mango	73.0
Raisins, golden	70.6
Zante currants	70.6
Raisins	65.0
Dates	64.2
Dried figs	62.3
Dried papaya	53.5
Dried pears	49.0
Dried peaches	44.6
Dried prunes	44.0
Dried apricots	38.9

FRESH FRUITS

Very High in Total Sugars	Total Sugars per 100 Grams
Grapes	18.1
Banana	15.6
Mango	14.8
Cherries, sweet	14.6

High in Total Sugars

Apple	13.3
Pineapple	11.9
Purple passion fruit	11.2

Moderate in Total Sugars

Kiwi	10.5
Pear	10.5
Pear, Bosc	10.5
Pear, Anjou	10.5
Pomegranate	10.1
Raspberries	9.5
Apricot	9.3
Orange	9.2
Watermelon	9.0
Cantaloupe	8.7
Peach	8.7
Nectarine	8.5
Jackfruit	8.4
Honeydew melon	8.2
Blackberries	8.1
Cherries, sour	8.1
Tangerine	7.7
Plum	7.5

Low in Total Sugars

Blueberries	7.3
Starfruit	7.1
Elderberries	7.0
Figs (fresh)	6.9
Mamey apple	6.5
Grapefruit, pink	6.2
Grapefruit, white	6.2
Guava	6.0
Guava, strawberry	6.0

Papaya	5.9
Strawberries	5.8
Casaba melon	4.7

Very Low in Total Sugars

Tomato	2.8
Lemon	2.5
Avocado, California	0.9
Avocado, Florida	0.9
Lime	0.4

Our List of Recommended Vegetables

Except for potatoes and corn, you can't go wrong with fresh veggies. Try to eat them at every meal, including breakfast. Why not fold some chopped scallions, avocado slices, and diced tomatoes into your next omelet, made with omega 3–enriched eggs? If you are obese or have signs and symptoms of metabolic syndrome, limit your servings of yams and sweet potatoes to one a day. Remember that peas and green beans are legumes, and these foods were rarely on Stone Age menus. Otherwise, enjoy these incredibly healthy foods.

- Artichoke
- Asparagus
- Beet greens
- Beets
- Bell peppers
- Broccoli
- Brussels sprouts
- Cabbage
- Carrots
- Cauliflower
- Celery
- Collards
- Cucumber
- Dandelion
- Eggplant
- Endive
- Green onions
- Kale
- Kohlrabi
- Lettuce
- Mushrooms
- Mustard greens

- Onions
- Parsley
- Parsnip
- Peppers
- Pumpkin
- Purslane
- Radish
- Rutabaga
- Seaweed
- Spinach
- Squash
- Sweet potatoes
- Swiss chard
- Tomatillos
- Tomato
- Turnip greens
- Turnips
- Watercress
- Yams

Nuts and Seeds

Nuts are rich sources of monounsaturated fats, which lower your blood cholesterol, thereby reducing your risk of heart disease and certain cancers, including breast cancer. However, because nuts and seeds are such concentrated sources of fat, they have the potential to slow down weight loss, particularly if you're overweight or obese. If you are, you should limit your consumption of nuts and seeds to less than 4 ounces per day. Once your metabolism has increased and you've reached your desired weight, you can eat more nuts, particularly walnuts, which have a more favorable omega 6 to omega 3 ratio than any other nut. Almost all nuts contain high concentrations of omega 6 fatty acids, and if eaten excessively can create an imbalance of fatty acids in your diet.

Peanuts are legumes, not nuts, and are absolutely not on the Paleo Diet menu. Peanuts contain substances that rapidly enter our bloodstreams and can promote allergies, autoimmune diseases, and heart disease. Nut allergies, particularly peanut and pine nut allergies, are common and can disrupt your health.

Here's our list of recommended nuts and seeds, but remember to listen to your body and let it be the final judge of what you should and shouldn't eat, particularly when it comes to nuts and seeds.

- Almonds
- Brazil nuts
- Cashews
- Chestnuts
- Hazelnuts (filberts)
- Macadamia nuts
- Pecans
- Pistachios (unsalted)
- Pumpkin seeds
- Sesame seeds
- Sunflower seeds
- Walnuts

For ideal health you should eat lots of lean meat, seafood, fish, and fresh fruits and vegetables with every meal along with moderate amounts of nuts, avocados, seeds, and healthful oils (olive, flaxseed, walnut, and avocado). Dried fruit should be consumed in small quantities because it causes rapid increases in blood glucose and insulin levels. When you're hungry or in doubt, start with a high-protein, low-fat food. Remember, lean protein is the most effective nutrient to reduce your appetite and boost your metabolism to help you burn stored fat and lose weight.

Vegetable and Cooking Oils

Vegetable oils were clearly not a component of Stone Age diets, simply because our hunter-gatherer ancestors did not have the technology to produce them. Oils made from walnuts, almonds, olives, sesame seeds, and flax seeds were initially manufactured using primitive presses about five to six thousand years ago. Nevertheless, except for olive oil, most early utilization of plant oils was for non-food purposes, such as lubrication, lighting, and medication. It wasn't until the start of the twentieth century, with the arrival of mechanically driven steel expellers and hexane extraction methods, that vegetable oils contributed noticeable calories to the Western diet.

Today the vegetable oils used in cooking, salad oils, margarine, shortening, and processed foods supply 17.6 percent of the total daily energy in the U.S. diet. This massive infusion of vegetable oils into our food supply starting in the early 1900s is to blame for elevating the dietary omega 6 to omega 3 ratio to its current and damaging value of ten to one. In hunter-gatherer diets, the omega 6 to omega 3 ratio was closer to two to one. Numerous diseases associated with this imbalance of fatty acids include heart disease, cancer, autoimmune diseases, metabolic syndrome, and almost all inflammatory diseases that end with "-itis". If we use the evolutionary model exclusively, then vegetable oils should constitute only a minimal part of contemporary Paleo diets.

If this is the case, then why not completely do away with all vegetable oils? I still believe that certain oils may be used in cooking and to add flavor to condiments, dressings, and marinades. Simply stated, there are at least four oils—flaxseed, walnut, olive, and avocado—that promote health and assist in getting the correct balance of good fats back into your diet.

Since the publication of the first edition of *The Paleo Diet* in 2002, I have reversed my position on canola oil and can no longer endorse its consumption. Canola oil comes from the seeds of the rape plant (*Brassica rapa* or *Brassica campestris*), which is a relative of the broccoli, cabbage, Brussels sprouts, and kale family. Undoubtedly, humans have eaten cabbage and its relatives since before historical times, and I still strongly support the consumption of these health-promoting vegetables. Nevertheless, the concentrated oil from *Brassica* seeds is another story.

In its original form, rape plants produced a seed oil that contained elevated levels (20 to 50 percent) of erucic acid (a monounsaturated fatty acid labeled 22:1n9). Erucic acid is toxic and causes tissue damage in many organs of laboratory animals. In the early 1970s, Canadian plant breeders developed a strain of rape plant that yielded a seed with less than 2 percent erucic acid (thus the name canola oil).

The erucic acid content of commercially available canola oil averages 0.6 percent. Despite its low erucic acid content, a number of experiments in the 1970s showed that even at low concentrations (2.0 and 0.88 percent), canola oil fed to rats could still elicit minor heart scarring that was considered pathological. A series of recent rat studies of low-erucic canola oil conducted by Dr. Ohara and colleagues at the Hatano Research Institute in Japan reported kidney injuries, increases in blood sodium levels, and abnormal changes in the hormone aldosterone, which regulates blood pressure.

Other harmful effects of canola oil consumption in animals (at 10 percent of their total calories) included decreased litter sizes, behavioral changes, and liver damage. A number of recent human studies of canola and rapeseed oil by Dr. Poiikonen and colleagues at the University of Tempere in Finland showed it to be a potent allergen in adults and children that causes allergic cross-reactions from other environmental allergens. Based on these brand-new findings in both humans and animals, I prefer to err on the safe side and can no longer recommend canola oil in the modern-day Paleo Diet.

Both olive oil and avocado oil are high (73.9 and 70.6 percent, respectively) in blood cholesterol–lowering monounsaturated fatty acids, but have less than positive omega 6 to omega 3 ratios of 11.7 and 13.5. Therefore, excessive consumption of both of these oils, without enough long-chain omega 3 fatty acids (EPA and DHA), will derail an otherwise healthy diet.

I recommend that you get 1.0 to 2.0 grams of EPA and DHA per day from either fish or fish oil capsules. Because avocado oil and macadamia oil are difficult to find and are expensive, this leaves olive oil as the staple for cooking, salad dressings, and marinades. If you can afford it, you should always choose extra virgin olive oil, as this grade of olive oil is produced by physical means, without chemical treatment and contains the highest concentration of polyphenolic compounds, which protect you from cancer, heart disease, and inflammation.

When you sauté, fry, or cook, I can recommend only olive oil. Most other vegetable oils decompose rapidly at high cooking temperatures and produce toxic, cancer-causing by-products. Sautéing means to cook quickly over moderately high heat in a small amount of fat. Stir-frying, in contrast, means to cook small uniform pieces of food by tossing them over high heat in a small amount of oil (never in butter). Two important points about sautéing foods: the olive oil in the pan must be very hot before you add the food to it, and the pan must not be crowded, or else the food will simmer rather than sauté.

Non-Paleo Foods to Eat in Moderation

We obviously no longer live in a Stone Age world; consequently, it is impossible to eat only the Stone Age foods that were available to our ancestors. However, a number of modern foods that you may enjoy have little or no detrimental effect on your health, particularly if they are consumed in moderation. Some people are surprised to discover that alcohol is in this category. There is no evidence that our Stone Age ancestors drank any form of alcoholic beverage. But it's abundantly clear in our own day that the abuse of alcohol—in addition to causing a host of severe behavioral and social problems—can impair your health, damage the liver, and increase your risk of developing many cancers.

If you currently drink in moderation or enjoy an occasional beer or glass of wine, there's no need to forgo this pleasure on the Paleo Diet. In fact, many scientific studies suggest that moderate alcohol consumption significantly reduces the risk of death from heart disease and other illnesses. Wine, in particular, when consumed in moderation, has been shown to have many favorable health effects. A glass of wine before or during dinner may help to improve your insulin sensitivity and reduce your hunger. Wine is also an appetizing ingredient that adds taste to many meat and vegetable dishes. Those with an autoimmune disease should avoid alcoholic beverages entirely, however, because alcohol increases intestinal permeability, an initial change that is known to precede the development of autoimmune diseases.

Here is a list of non-Paleo foods of which you may partake, but make sure you don't overdo them.

OILS
- Olive, avocado, walnut, or flaxseed oil (use in moderation—4 tablespoons or less a day when weight loss is of primary importance)

BEVERAGES
- Diet sodas (These often contain artificial sweeteners such as aspartame and saccharine, which may be harmful; you're better off drinking bottled and mineral waters.)
- Coffee
- Tea
- Wine (two 4-ounce glasses). Don't buy "cooking wine," which is loaded with salt.
- Beer (one 12-ounce serving)
- Hard liquor (4 ounces)

"STONE AGE" SWEETS
- Dried fruits (no more than 2 ounces a day, particularly if you are trying to lose weight)
- Nuts mixed with dried and fresh fruit (no more than 4 ounces of nuts and 2 ounces of dried fruit a day, particularly if you are trying to lose weight)

Foods You Should Avoid

We've spent a considerable amount of time dealing with why the foods in the following list should not be part of your new Paleo menu. Keep in mind the 85-15 rule as you gradually purge these non-Paleo foods from your diet.

DAIRY FOODS

- All processed foods made with any dairy products
- Butter
- Cheese
- Cream
- Dairy spreads
- Frozen yogurt
- Ice cream
- Ice milk
- Whole milk
- Skim milk, low-fat milk
- Nonfat dairy creamer
- Powdered milk
- Yogurt

CEREAL GRAINS

- Barley (barley soup, barley bread, and all processed foods made with barley)
- Corn (corn on the cob, corn tortillas, corn chips, cornstarch, corn syrup)
- Millet
- Oats (steel-cut oats, rolled oats, and all processed foods made with oats)
- Rice (brown rice, white rice, ramen, rice noodles, basmati rice, rice cakes, rice flour, and all processed foods made with rice)
- Rye (rye bread, rye crackers, and all processed foods made with rye)
- Sorghum
- Wheat (bread, rolls, muffins, noodles, crackers, cookies, cake, doughnuts, pancakes, waffles, pasta, spaghetti, lasagna, wheat tortillas, pizza, pita bread, flat bread, and all processed foods made with wheat or wheat flour)
- Wild rice

CEREAL-GRAINLIKE SEEDS

- Amaranth
- Buckwheat
- Quinoa

LEGUMES

- All beans (adzuki beans, black beans, broad beans, fava beans, field beans, garbanzo beans, horse beans, kidney beans, lima beans, mung beans, navy beans, pinto beans, red beans, string beans, white beans)

- Black-eyed peas
- Chickpeas
- Lentils
- Peas
- Miso
- Peanut butter
- Peanuts (peanuts are a legume and not a nut)
- Snow peas
- Soybeans and all soybean products, including tofu

STARCHY TUBERS
- Potatoes and all potato products

SALT-CONTAINING FOODS
- Almost all commercial salad dressings and condiments
- Bacon
- Cheeses
- Deli meats
- Frankfurters
- Ham
- Salami
- Hot dogs
- Ketchup
- Olives
- Pickled foods
- Pork rinds
- Salted nuts
- Salted spices
- Virtually all canned meats and fish
- Sausages
- Processed meats
- Smoked, dried, and salted fish and meat

FATTY MEATS
- All fatty cuts of fresh meats
- Fatty pork chops
- Fatty pork roasts
- Pork ribs
- Bacon
- Pork sausage
- Beef ribs
- Fatty leg of lamb
- Fatty lamb roasts
- Lamb chops
- Chicken and turkey legs
- Chicken and turkey thighs and wings
- Fatty beef roasts
- T-bone steaks
- Fatty cuts of beef
- Fatty ground beef

- All sugary soft drinks
- Canned, bottled, and freshly squeezed juices and fruit drinks

- Candy
- Sugars
- Honey

Autoimmune Diseases and the Paleo Diet

Why are we talking about autoimmune diseases in a cookbook? It's very simple. You, and every other cook in the world, have a huge influence upon the health and well-being of everyone you prepare meals for, including your family and yourself. The kitchen and the cook can be the centerpiece of joyful lives filled with vigor, longevity, and freedom from disease. By choosing healthy, delicious, "real" foods, you have the power to impact the destiny of your family's health and your own, including freedom from cancer, heart disease, and autoimmune diseases.

You may not know it, but after cardiovascular disease and cancer, autoimmune diseases are the most common class of illnesses in the United States, afflicting between 14.7 to 23.5 million people, or 5 to 8 percent of the population. Commonly recognized autoimmune diseases, such as ulcerative colitis, multiple sclerosis, and rheumatoid arthritis, develop when the body's immune system loses the ability to distinguish between what is "self" and what is "nonself," attacking healthy tissues and organs as if they were foreign invaders.

In the case of ulcerative colitis, strong immune responses are directed against specific proteins in the colon. With multiple sclerosis, the sheaths that cover the nerves are destroyed. In rheumatoid arthritis, the joints are attacked by the immune system. More than a hundred specific diseases are known to be autoimmune in nature, and you will probably recognize a few of the more common ones listed in the table below.

One of the surprising facts about autoimmune diseases is that environmental elements represent 70 percent of the risk for developing these illnesses. Genetics play a lesser role, with 30 percent of the risk being attributed to inherited factors. Up until the last five to ten years, autoimmune diseases were the black boxes of the medical world. We really had no idea how or why environmental factors triggered these diseases in genetically susceptible people.

Some astonishing developments have occurred in the past five years, particularly from Dr. Alessio Fasano at the University of

THE MOST COMMON AUTOIMMUNE DISEASES

Disease	Tissue or Organ Affected	Prevalence
Alopecia areata	Hair follicle	170 per 100,000
Ankylosing spondylitis	Spine and sacroiliac joints	129 per 100,000
Autoimmune uticaria	Skin	330 per 100,000
Celiac disease	Small intestine	400 per 100,000
Crohn's disease	Gastrointestinal tract	184 per 100,000
Diabetes, type 1	Pancreas	120 per 100,000
Graves' disease	Thyroid gland	1,120 per 100,000
Hashimoto's thyroiditis	Thyroid gland	9,460 per 100,000
Lupus erythematosus	Any tissue in the body	510 per 100,000
Multiple sclerosis	Brain, nerves	140 per 100,000
Psoriasis	Skin	2,020 per 100,000
Rheumatoid arthritis	Joints	920 per 100,000
Scleroderma	Skin, other organs	110 per 100,000
Ulcerative colitis	Colon	35–100 per 100,000
Uveitis	Anterior eye	850 per 100,000
Vitiligo	Skin	740 per 100,000

Maryland Center for Celiac Research, that have helped to unravel the mysteries underlying autoimmune diseases. Work from Dr. Fasano's group, as well as from other scientists worldwide, shows that a "leaky gut," or increased intestinal permeability, plays a crucial initial step in triggering some, if not all, autoimmune diseases.

Amazingly, wheat—consumed by almost every person on the planet—has been found to be one of the primary culprits underlying leaky gut, not just in autoimmune patients, but also in healthy people. Wheat contains a protein called gliadin, which interacts with gut receptors to set off a cascade of hormonal events ultimately allowing the intestinal contents (food and bacteria) to interact with the immune system. Withdrawal of wheat from celiac patients completely cures disease symptoms, and scientific evidence increasingly shows that this strategy may work for other autoimmune diseases, including type 1 diabetes, if it is caught early.

Dr. Fasano's finding doesn't really affect Paleo Dieters, because all grains, including wheat, have never been part of the menu. However, since the discovery that a leaky gut most likely represents a necessary first step in the development of autoimmunity, it has become clear to me and my scientific colleagues that any dietary element capable of increasing intestinal permeability should also be suspect in autoimmune diseases. As we pored over the scientific literature, we discovered the following list of foods and substances, in addition to gliadin in wheat, that promote a leaky gut:

- Alcohol
- Nonsteroidal anti-inflammatory drugs (NSAIDs): aspirin, ibuprofen, naproxen
- Oral contraceptives
- Antacids containing aluminum hydroxide (alum)
- Capsaicin-containing chili peppers
- Certain saponin- or glycoalkaloid-containing foods
- Certain lectin-containing foods

At first glance, this list doesn't seem to be very impressive, as you may not recognize all the common foods that contain lectins, saponins, and glycoalkaloids. So let me be a little more up-front and point out these problematic foods.

Let's start with lectins. Almost all grains and legumes contain lectins, most of which increase intestinal permeability. Because the Paleo Diet has always been a grain-free and legume-free diet, there really is nothing new here, except that now we are beginning to understand why the Paleo Diet has such potent therapeutic and curative powers for autoimmune patients: it is virtually free of the lectins known to increase intestinal permeability.

The most recent twist to the Paleo Diet and autoimmune diseases involves saponins, toxic compounds found in many plants that ward off microbial and insect attacks. Unfortunately, saponins are bad news not only for insects and microbes, which try to eat them, but also for humans. If we eat saponins in large enough amounts, they can become lethally toxic. Even at low doses they may cause a leaky gut. Beans (legumes) and soy products are concentrated sources of gut-permeating saponins. Once again, this is why the Paleo Diet is such good medicine for autoimmune patients, as these foods have never been part of the Paleo Diet.

When I wrote *The Paleo Diet* eight years ago, I advised you not to eat potatoes, mainly because of their high glycemic load, which adversely affects blood sugar and insulin levels. It turns out that this recommendation is also good advice for people with autoimmune diseases. I now know that potatoes contain two specific saponins called glycoalkaloids (alpha solanine and alpha chaconine), which increase intestinal permeability. Eliminating potatoes from your diet not only prevents blood glucose and insulin surges but also helps to prevent a leaky gut and autoimmune diseases.

Paleo Diets are good therapy for people with autoimmune diseases because they are devoid of lectin-containing grains, lectin- and saponin-containing legumes, and saponin- and lectin-containing potatoes. Do your gut a favor and kick these foods out of your diet. While you are at it, make sure you also avoid milk and dairy products, per my original recommendations in *The Paleo Diet*. Epidemiological (population) studies have frequently implicated milk and dairy foods in numerous autoimmune diseases, including type 1 diabetes, rheumatoid arthritis, and multiple sclerosis. Furthermore, experimental studies have demonstrated that certain cow milk proteins can actually cause the animal equivalent of multiple sclerosis in rats. Because the Paleo Diet is devoid of dairy, grains, legumes, and potatoes, it's no wonder it's such good medicine for people with autoimmune diseases.

Besides contributing to a leaky gut, certain dietary saponins agitate the immune system in a manner that makes it much more likely to cause autoimmune diseases. Saponins have long been used by immunologists to boost the effectiveness of vaccines in revving up the immune system. So the bottom line is, if you have an autoimmune disease, you should avoid saponins.

In addition to legumes and potatoes, other commonly consumed foods containing saponins that may contribute to a leaky gut include green tomatoes, alfalfa sprouts, quinoa, amaranth, and soft drinks containing the additive quillaja. A final note of caution for autoimmune patients: avoid hot chili peppers, hot sauces, and salsas. These foods contain high concentrations of capsaicin, another food element that increases intestinal permeability.

2

Paleo Kitchen Guidelines

Whether you are new to cooking or a seasoned chef, learning to create Paleo dishes will take some adjustments to your thinking, as you incorporate brand-new food preparation techniques and concepts into Paleo healthy eating. In this chapter, we make it easy for you to quickly set up your kitchen, acquire the important tools, and clean out and restock your fridge and pantry so that you may begin to discover the amazing and rewarding health benefits awaiting you on this lifetime journey into Paleo living.

When first introduced to the Paleo Diet concept, many newbies often begin by wondering whether they will miss some of the foods that are not on the Paleo menu. The best advice we can give is for you to focus on the incredible wealth of delicious and vitamin-, nutrient- and protein-packed real foods the Paleo Diet has to offer. You will not be deprived or hungry. Soon your taste buds will reawaken to the subtle tastes and textures of soothing fruits, crisp vegetables, succulent lean meats, and savory seafood.

Use your imagination and creativity to make your ancestral diet work for you. Explore the endless possibilities real food has to offer, as you replace your old, unhealthy, processed foods with exciting, new, good-for-you Paleo cuisine. We're sure that like most Paleo Dieters, you will soon lose your cravings for artificially salty, sugary, synthetic, processed foods and quickly develop a preference for the foods you were genetically designed to eat. Let's get started.

Cleaning Out the Kitchen

The kitchen should be your starting point as you transition into a Paleo lifestyle. Rest assured, if it comes in a plastic bag, a box, a can, or a bottle, it's probably not Paleo-friendly; however, there are a few key exceptions, which we will get to later.

Any food, even non-Paleo foods that you have purchased with your hard-earned cash, can be difficult to part with. However psychologically difficult it may be, it is still better not to tempt yourself by finishing up the last half gallon of ice cream in your refrigerator or the final bag of chips in your pantry. Get rid of them—put them out of sight and out of mind. We are not asking you to waste this food entirely but rather to jettison it from your life. Think about your purging of old foods as the first step on a journey to improved health, athletic performance, and vigor; better sleep; and a longer life, free of medications.

What to Toss from the Pantry

Let's start with the pantry (and/or kitchen cabinets), since this is where most people store huge supplies of non-Paleo food. If your pantry is similar to most others, you've got a lot of cleaning out to do. We suggest that you get some large cardboard boxes, fill them up with the discarded foods, and donate these items to your local food bank or charity. These organizations will gladly accept any and all unopened packages, cans, or bottles, and you can even get a tax write-off for your generosity. However, partly used foods or opened containers must either be thrown out or given to friends or neighbors.

A good starting point is foods that contain wheat, sugar, or salt. If the food item in question contains any of these ingredients, it immediately goes into your donation box. This initial step will probably eliminate about 75 percent of the articles in your pantry.

The next items up for clearance are grains or any processed foods made with grains. Out goes your box of instant rice; out go the so-called healthy brown or basmati rice, wild rice, and rice cakes. Out go corn meal, cornflakes, corn chips, and taco shells. Don't forget rye, barley, and oats. That big box of oatmeal should be ditched, along with your rye crisp crackers and granola bars. Other taboo grains or grainlike foods include millet, bulghur, couscous, quinoa, amaranth, and buckwheat. Potatoes—in any way, shape, or form—must exit your pantry. This means potato chips, Pringles, dehydrated mashed potatoes, shoestring potatoes, and any other potato-containing product.

The easy discards are cookies, crackers, chips, candies, and salty canned foods. But how about your canned tuna, salmon, and sardines? These are expensive, high-protein foods that are rich in the healthy omega 3 fatty acids. What should you do with them? Our suggestion is to keep these for later use in salads, omelets, or other dishes. Canned tuna and salmon are usually packed in salt water, so place them in a colander and rinse thoroughly to remove the salt.

Unfortunately, canned fish and seafood also contain high amounts of oxidized cholesterol, a substance that promotes artery clogging and heart disease. Consequently, fresh or frozen fish is almost always a better choice. The lackluster, leached-out, salty flavor of canned tuna can't hold a candle to the savory, pungent overtones of broiled fresh yellowfin or blue tuna—and tuna steaks are also more nutritious for you than canned tuna. Let your new Paleo palate become your guide to unadulterated, fresh foods, as Mother Nature always intended.

Other items that should be thrown out of your pantry are commercial salad dressings, mustard, ketchup, salsa, pickles, barbecue sauce, and tomato sauce, because of their high salt, sugar, and omega 6 fatty acid content. Almost all vegetable, salad, and cooking oils, except those we recommended in chapter 1, should also be relegated to the discard box.

How about coconut oil? Coconut oil, meat, and milk are traditional foods of tropical islanders living close to the world's oceans and seas. These foods are concentrated sources of lauric acid, a saturated fat that elevates blood cholesterol levels and increases the risk for cardiovascular disease in Western populations. Strangely enough, traditional cultures that consume coconut foods have little or no heart disease, stroke, or other cardiovascular problems normally associated with eating saturated fats (such as the lauric acid found in coconuts).

Although we don't completely understand this inconsistency, it may be due to lauric acid's positive antibacterial effect in the gut. Lauric acid from coconut foods may protect your heart and blood vessels from cardiovascular disease by reducing those gut bacteria that increase intestinal permeability, a known risk factor for heart disease because of chronic, low-level systemic inflammation. Based on the evidence of traditional Pacific Islanders, coconut oil, meat, and milk do not increase your risk for cardio-vascular disease, particularly as part of a modern Paleo Diet. So let your palate "go back to the islands" and enjoy the delicious health benefits of this time-honored plant food.

One final recommendation for your pantry: get rid of all beans, lentils, dried peas, peanuts, and legumes. These foods were not found in early human diets simply because they are inedible unless cooked. Humans have been on the planet for about two and a half million years, but the controlled use of fire is quite recent: only about three hundred thousand years old. So our species has had little evolutionary time to adapt to a family of foods that are concentrated sources of certain antinutrients (lectins, phytates, protease inhibitors, and saponins) that increase intestinal perme-ability, promote chronic systemic inflammation, and adversely affect our health.

What to Toss from the Refrigerator

Now that you have tossed the unhealthy foods from your pantry, let's take time to explore your fridge and see the lurking food dangers herein. Like most people living in the United States, Europe, Canada, Australia, and other Westernized societies, your fridge probably contains a few bottles or cartons of pasteurized homoge-nized milk from your local store or dairy, some yogurt, a few sticks of butter, and a variety of cheeses, to say nothing of frozen dairy foods (such as ice cream, ice milk, and frozen yogurt). Although these foods constitute about 10 percent of the calories in the typ-ical U.S. diet, they were entirely absent from our Stone Age ances-tors' menu. X-ray studies of dairy-free hunter-gatherer skeletons show these people had healthy, robust bones free of osteoporosis. If you get sufficient fresh fruits and veggies (around 35 percent of your calories) in your contemporary Paleo Diet and just a little sunlight, calcium and dairy products become a nonissue.

Your refrigerator also probably contains a variety of non-Paleo processed foods, which could never have composed even a small percentage of humanity's original diet. For instance, frozen concentrated juices such as lemonade, apple juice, grape juice, and orange juice have to be cleaned out, as these are all high-glycemic-load foods that spike your blood sugar level. As with your pantry, a good rule of thumb is: if it contains wheat, salt, or sugar, dump it. If you have frozen fruit or veggies, keep them. However, after they are finished, try to always get the fresh versions—they are healthier and they taste better.

Most non-Paleo refrigerators are loaded with artificial processed meats such as bacon, sausage, salami, bologna, lunch meats, and others. Although you may have paid dearly for these meats, remember that they are laced with salt, nitrites, nitrates, sugar, by-products, and other unhealthy additives. So do yourself a favor and pitch these artificial creations. Finally, check your frozen meat section. If you have fatty feedlot-produced meats, keep them. But next time, try to buy grass-fed meats or the leaner cuts of commercial meats.

Non-Paleo Foods Checklist

As you scour your kitchen, you'll be amazed at the amount of unhealthy foods you've accumulated. Most of the items to be purged will be obvious, while others are not so clear-cut. Use the following comprehensive guide if you have any doubts. Finally, don't forget to check the labels on any vitamins or supplements you may be taking for any non-Paleo ingredients.

DAIRY FOODS

- All processed foods made with any dairy products
- Butter
- Cheese
- Cream
- Dairy spreads
- Frozen yogurt
- Ice cream

- Ice milk
- Whole milk
- Skim milk, low-fat milk
- Nonfat dairy creamer
- Powdered milk
- Yogurt
- Whey protein powders

CEREAL GRAINS

- Barley: barley soup, barley bread, and all processed foods made with barley
- Corn: corn on the cob, corn tortillas, corn chips, cornstarch, corn syrup
- Millet
- Oats: steel-cut oats, rolled oats, and all processed foods made with oats
- Rice: brown rice, white rice, wild rice, ramen, rice noodles, basmati rice, rice cakes, rice flour, and all processed foods made with rice
- Rye: rye bread, rye crackers, and all processed foods made with rye
- Sorghum
- Wheat (bread, rolls, muffins, noodles, crackers, cookies, cake, doughnuts, pancakes, waffles, pasta, spaghetti, lasagna, wheat tortillas, pizza, pita bread, flat bread, and all processed foods made with wheat or wheat flour)
- Bulghur (cracked wheat)
- Couscous
- All grain-based flours, including gluten-free flours

CEREAL-GRAINLIKE SEEDS

- Amaranth
- Buckwheat
- Chia seeds
- Quinoa

LEGUMES

- All beans: adzuki beans, black beans, broad beans, fava beans, field beans, garbanzo beans (chickpeas), green beans, horse beans, kidney beans, lima beans, mung beans, navy beans, pinto beans, red beans, string beans, white beans

Legumes (continued)

- Lentils
- Peanuts, peanut butter, peanut oil (peanuts are a legume and not a nut). Be particularly diligent when reading labels; even packaged mixed nuts labeled as peanut-free sometimes still contain peanut oil.
- All peas: black-eyed peas, green peas, snow peas, split peas
- Soybeans and all soy products: tofu, fresh or frozen edamame, miso, tempeh, soy sauce, tamari, ponzu, soy milk, soybean oil, and soy protein powders

STARCHY TUBERS

- Potatoes and all potato products

SALT-CONTAINING FOODS

- Almost all commercial salad dressings and condiments
- Bacon
- Cheese
- Deli meat
- Lunch meat
- Frankfurters
- Ham
- Salami
- Hot dogs
- Ketchup
- Olives
- Pickles and pickled foods
- Pork rinds
- Salted nuts
- Salted spices
- Virtually all canned meats and fish
- Sausage
- Any other processed meat
- Smoked, dried, and salted fish and meat

FATTY MEATS

- All fatty cuts of fresh meat
- Fatty pork chops
- Fatty pork roast
- Pork ribs
- Bacon
- Pork sausage
- Fatty leg of lamb
- Fatty lamb roast

- Fatty lamb chops
- Chicken and turkey drumsticks, thighs, and wings
- Beef ribs
- Fatty beef roast
- T-bone steak
- Fatty cuts of beef
- Fatty ground beef

- All sugary soft drinks
- Freshly squeezed fruit or vegetable drinks (okay only for athletes)
- Canned or bottled fruit drinks
- All frozen fruit juices
- Popsicles

- Candy
- Chocolate
- Honey
- Molasses
- Corn syrup
- All refined sugars, including maple syrup, date sugar, and any product that contains fructose, sucrose, or glucose

- All vinegars and foods containing vinegar
- Foods containing artificial colors or flavors
- Foods containing preservatives
- All spice blends containing salt
- Vitamin supplements containing rice starch, soy, wheat, and other grain-based ingredients

Restocking Your Kitchen with Paleo Staples

When most of us think about stocking the pantry, we imagine loading it up with staples that won't spoil. This bias comes from an earlier era, before refrigeration, when it was necessary to keep large supplies of flour, sugar, dried rice, beans, and canned goods on hand. Fresh fruits and vegetables were seasonal luxuries, not staples. Refrigeration and international air travel have now made it possible to eat our ancestral diet no matter where we live.

Once you have purged your shelves of your former staples, you will be amazed at the amount of shelf space that is freed up. You have now successfully completed the first step in your kitchen's Paleo makeover and are ready to begin the fun process of stocking up on the true necessities for Paleo cooking.

Paleo Pantry Staples

You will soon discover that certain items are essential to have in your newly revised pantry at all times. The convenience and longer shelf life of these items will allow you to quickly and easily prepare Paleo meals without having to run to the store every day. As you can see, except for spices and starchy root vegetables, little or no pantry space is required in Paleo kitchens, because "real food" is fresh food, which typically must be refrigerated. Note that the items in the following list are not necessarily comprehensive, but they are key ingredients in day-to-day Paleo cooking.

OILS

- Extra virgin olive oil
- Walnut oil
- Avocado oil
- Macadamia oil
- Coconut oil

RAW NUTS

- Almonds
- Brazil nuts
- Hazelnuts (filberts)
- Pecans
- Walnuts

- Allspice
- Anise
- Basil
- Bay leaf
- Cayenne pepper
- Chili powder
- Cinnamon
- Cloves
- Cumin
- Curry powder
- Dill
- Garlic powder
- Ginger powder
- Nutmeg
- Onion powder
- Oregano
- Paprika
- Parsley
- Peppercorns, black. Always use fresh peppercorns and a good pepper mill rather than preground black pepper. There is no comparison.
- Rosemary
- Sage
- Thyme
- Turmeric

STARCHY ROOT VEGETABLE

- Sweet potatoes or yams

DRIED PROTEIN POWDER

- Powdered egg whites

Fresh Paleo Staples

While the following foods are not items you'd want to keep indefinitely in the refrigerator, buying them every week or two will allow you to keep things fresh, safe, and ready for use at a moment's notice. Keep in mind that these basics are listed not because they are nutritionally superior to all other Paleo foods but because they are familiar to most people and offer versatility while preparing fresh, healthy meals. See chapter 1 for more comprehensive food lists.

OIL

- Flaxseed oil

FRESH HERBS AND SPICES

- Basil
- Chives
- Cilantro
- Dill
- Parsley
- Tarragon

VEGETABLES

- Bell pepper
- Broccoli
- Carrots
- Cauliflower
- Celery
- Cucumber
- Lettuce
- Mushrooms
- Onions
- Radishes
- Scallions
- Spinach

FRESH FRUITS

Most fruits do not require refrigeration, but except for bananas, they may be kept cold to extend their shelf life. Feel free to branch out from the basics listed below and try more exotic fruits like papaya, guava, starfruit, passion fruit, dragon fruit, or African cucumber.

- Apple
- Avocado
- Banana
- Cantaloupe
- Grapes
- Grapefruit
- Lemon
- Orange
- Strawberries
- Tomato

MEAT, SEAFOOD, AND EGGS

We find ourselves replacing these staples on a weekly basis. For more information about purchasing, cooking, and preparing wholesome meat, eggs, and seafood, see chapter 1.

- Omega 3 eggs
- Fresh fish
- Fresh shellfish
- Free-range chicken
- Grass-fed beef

Kitchen Tools

Preparing your kitchen for healthy foods requires proper tools. To get you started, we have compiled a list of indispensable utensils, appliances, and paraphernalia that will make Paleo preparation and cooking a breeze. However, just as you purged your kitchen of food items, you must also eliminate certain non-Paleo utensils.

First, get rid of all pots, pans, vessels, and cookie sheets that have an aluminum surface. If aluminum touches the food during cooking, preparation, or dining, pitch these utensils. When you cook in aluminum pots or pans, small amounts of aluminum leach into your food and eventually find their way into your body, which is not a good thing. Although we don't completely understand how aluminum adversely affects human health and well-being, a number of studies suggest that it may impair the intestinal barrier, thereby promoting chronic low-level inflammation. Aluminum also seems to preferentially bind to nerve tissue and the brain. Whether it impairs cognition or nerve function is still unclear. We recommend that you replace all of your aluminum pots, pans, and cooking vessels with either stainless steel or Pyrex. It will be money well spent.

Along these same lines, do yourself a favor and replace your plastic water bottles, storage jugs, or plastic containers with stainless steel or glass (not aluminum). Besides polluting the world, plastic containers frequently contain BPA (bisphenol A), dioxins, and phthalates, which can leach into the liquids or foods that are stored in the containers. These chemicals may adversely affect your health and well-being in numerous ways.

One of the most indispensable items in a well-stocked Paleo kitchen is good cutlery. High-quality stainless steel knives can save you hours in cutting, chopping, and preparation time. If you don't already own first-rate cutlery, consider it a lifetime investment for your health and that of your family. Look for high-quality stainless steel knife sets that retain their edge, with sufficient knives to allow you the freedom to chop, cut, slice, or core any Paleo food.

ESSENTIALS

- 2-cup Pyrex measuring cup
- 4-quart stainless steel saucepan
- Stainless steel steaming basket
- 6-quart stainless steel stockpot
- 12-inch cast iron skillet
- Garlic press
- Glass or ceramic baking dishes
- Set of quality chef's knives
- Food processor, small (3-cup)
- Food thermometer
- Fruit and vegetable peeler
- Set of stainless steel measuring spoons
- Ceramic, glass, or stainless steel mixing bowls: small, medium, and large
- Spatulas
- Wooden spoons
- Two wooden cutting boards: one for raw meats, poultry, and fish and another for fruits and vegetables
- Blender
- Wire whisk

OPTIONAL (helpful and fun)

- Citrus juicer
- Digital food scale

- Kitchen mixer with meat grinder attachment
- Large food processor
- Mortar and pestle
- Mandoline food slicer
- Dehydrator, or food dryer
- Nut grinder

Cooking Temperatures

If you find yourself a bit worried about eating or serving raw or undercooked meat, poultry, or fish, a food thermometer works wonders. Use the following chart as your guideline.

USDA RECOMMENDED SAFE MINIMUM
INTERNAL TEMPERATURES

Dish	Recommended Internal Temperature (°F)
Steaks and roasts	145
Fish	145
Pork	160
Ground beef	160
Egg dishes	160
Chicken breasts	165
Whole poultry	165

All ovens vary, so use your food thermometer as the final decision maker when you're following our recipes. As you become familiar with your oven or grill, try to develop a sense of the time required to safely cook meat and fish. Some of our recipes include instructions to "tent" before serving. Tenting is a method of stopping food from browning too quickly in the oven. It is typically used in cooking a turkey but can also be employed with almost any dish that is cooked in the oven. It's sort of like putting a makeshift lid of aluminum foil over a food dish that doesn't otherwise have one. Tenting allows foods to continue cooking at cooler temperatures without burning.

A Sanitary Kitchen

It may sound trivial or even clichéd, but proper hand washing is crucial to prevent bacterial contamination and potential food poisoning. Keep a bottle of hand-pump soap next to your kitchen sink and use it regularly. Equally important is keeping work surfaces clean and sanitary to avoid cross-contamination. Use one cutting board for meats, fish, and poultry, and another for fruits and veggies. Plastic cutting boards tend to harbor bacteria and are more difficult to keep sanitized than wooden chopping blocks, which naturally discourage bacterial overgrowth and subsequent food contamination. Even still, every few weeks, you should sterilize your cutting board by dousing it with a thin layer of bleach for about five minutes and then thoroughly rinsing it.

Try to clean up simultaneously while you're cooking and preparing foods. It makes your final cleanup tasks a lot easier and ensures a healthy meal without the risk of contamination or food poisoning. Make it a habit to rinse and cut fish and meat in separate areas from fruits and veggies. Wash your hands frequently as you move from one food to another. Be sure to keep knives and utensils separate as well, not just for the preliminary preparation steps but also for cooking and serving.

Fundamental in keeping a safe and sanitary kitchen is your refrigerator. Raw fish and meat should be kept in a separate location from fresh fruits and veggies. Store eggs on the interior shelves, rather than on the door, where the temperature frequently is not quite cool enough to keep them safe. Take advantage of the crisper drawer to store leafy greens and other veggies in sealed plastic bags, which will double their shelf lives. A few times a month, or when necessary, wash the interior of your refrigerator with warm soapy water. Once a week, try to discard any food that looks past its prime or is starting to wilt or spoil. Although fresh is always better for you than frozen, it is impractical and expensive to eat fresh fish, meat, and poultry every day. Take advantage of sales and buy these foods in bulk. Divide them into meal-sized portions and freeze them in sealable plastic bags. These simple steps will go a long way in preventing spoilage or contamination of meat, fish, and poultry.

Budgeting Paleo Diets

Do you find yourself pining for grass-fed filet mignon only to be turned away by the twenty-eight dollars per pound price tag? Don't worry; with a little creativity and imagination, even those on a tight budget can stay true to their Paleo roots. The following tips will help get you started.

BUY IN BULK

- Raw nuts, dried herbs and spices, and even herbal teas can be purchased in large quantities from the bin or bulk section of your local grocery store or supermarket. This not only saves money but is eco-friendly because it reduces unnecessary packaging.
- Take advantage of poultry, meat, and fish specials and sales. For most single people, the refrigerator's freezer section is just fine. You can store enough frozen meat, fish, and poultry to last a few weeks. If you have a large family, consider buying a dedicated freezer.
- When fruits and vegetables go on sale, buy a large quantity and choose recipes that will maximize their use during the week. For instance, serve spaghetti squash with marinara sauce when tomatoes go on sale or make a big batch of

fresh salsa. With a little planning, you can take advantage of sale prices while preparing delicious meals for your family.

- Buy whole meat rather than precut, skinned, and boned selections. You can easily skin a chicken breast yourself and save quite a bit on the price. Similarly, take advantage of the lower price per pound of large roasts and simply slice them into smaller, more convenient portions, which you can then freeze.

BUY LOCALLY GROWN FOODS

- Let your food and meal choices be influenced by local and seasonal availability. Locally grown foods are almost always less expensive than their foreign counterparts. You also reduce your carbon footprint when you buy food from farmers' markets and local grocers.
- Be flexible with recipes and modify them to accommodate locally grown foods. Many of our recipes have plenty of room for improvisation and ingredient substitutions. Don't be afraid to try something new by making practical adaptations.

DO IT YOURSELF

- Do you love almond butter but not the seventeen dollars per jar price tag on the raw, organic variety? Investing in a small nut grinder might be worth your while. Buying nuts in bulk and grinding them yourself can result in delicious new blends. Walnut butter spread on celery sticks makes a quick and easy Paleo snack.
- Another great money-saving idea is to make your own jerky, dried fish, or dried meat. Home dehydrators are inexpensive and can also be used to make dried fruits and veggies. Dried banana slices are delectable.

- Start a little backyard garden. Find out which fruits, vegetables, and herbs grow well in your climate and locale. Nothing beats homegrown baby lettuce, radishes, tomatoes, and scallions, and these can be grown just about anywhere. You even can set aside a small part of your yard for strawberries, raspberries, blackberries, and blueberries; these also grow well in most climates.
- Start a food cooperative in your neighborhood. You might grow basil, oregano, and rosemary. Your neighbor will grow tomatoes, while someone across the street will cultivate squash. Before you know it, everybody benefits as your garden-fresh fruits and veggies mature and are harvested throughout the summer and fall.

Choose Organic Wisely

Should you spend your hard-earned money on organic produce? Are there any health or nutritional benefits to it? The scientific literature generally has shown that except for a slightly higher vitamin C content in organically produced vegetables (but not fruit), no differences could be demonstrated for any other vitamins or minerals. So if you're considering buying organic produce for its greater nutrient content, it's just not worth it.

However, one important difference that does stand out between organic and conventional produce is in the levels of nitrate. Nitrate concentrations in organic fruits and veggies are consistently lower than in conventional produce. By and large, neither conventional nor organic produce exceeds nitrate limits established by the World Health Organization and the Environmental Protection Agency.

Organic produce also usually contains lower pesticide levels than generic supermarket produce. Because increased environmental and dietary exposure to both nitrates and pesticides is associated with an elevated risk for developing certain cancers, you may want to consider going organic.

Reinvent Leftovers

There are no hard and fast rules when dealing with leftovers. Use your creativity to turn last night's dinner into tomorrow's new and exciting dishes. Have you prepared too much turkey for tonight's dinner? Put it in the fridge, and tomorrow evening dice it and add some curry powder, olive oil, a handful of raisins, and some chopped apple, and you've created a sumptuous turkey salad to enjoy on a bed of mixed greens.

Finding novel and creative ways to keep Paleo dining at the center of your healthy lifestyle is the goal. Try to get your friends and relatives involved. Invite the kids, your spouse, or your roommate along as you plan, prepare, and cook Paleo meals. Join various Internet Paleo support groups, trade recipes, visit ethnic markets to find brand-new ingredients, or even take up hunting and fishing. By establishing and maintaining Paleo eating habits, you'll guarantee yourself and your family a lifetime of good health and well-being.

3

Paleo Breakfasts

Paleo breakfasts may take a little while getting used to, because they generally are quite different from what you may be accustomed to. But don't let these differences worry you; our Stone Age ancestors' food choices for breakfast are exactly what we need in our modern world to maintain even energy all morning long and reduce our risk of numerous chronic diseases. Morning meals for our Paleo ancestors were based on more than two and a half million years of evolutionary wisdom, and current studies of hunter-gatherers show that if they ate breakfast at all, it was typically a little bit of yesterday's kill.

If you are like most Americans, you are used to a breakfast that is a high-carbohydrate meal including some sort of cereal (oatmeal, boxed cereal with milk, bagel, sweet roll, buttered toast, pancakes, waffles.), with coffee and fruit juice. The other option for "born in the USA" breakfasts is a high-fat, stick-to-your-ribs meal consisting of bacon, sausage, or ham with eggs and hash-brown potatoes.

Salmon steaks and chicken breasts usually aren't on very many breakfast menus, but they should be. Paleo morning meals were typically high in protein and low in carbohydrate and fat and consisted of leftovers from the animal that was killed earlier. Accordingly, a common breakfast for Paleo Dieters might be slices of cold London broil or cold crab legs (left over from last night's dinner), and half of a cantaloupe or a bowl of fresh straw-berries.

As we get more and more into this way of eating, many of us eat not only meat and fish for breakfast but also veggies. It's not so unusual to eat onions, bell peppers, and chopped tomatoes in your omelet, but broccoli or asparagus spears as a side dish may sound a bit odd at first. However, it is entirely our cultural biases and not our nutritional needs that have determined our idea of a suitable breakfast. So go ahead—try fish or meat first thing in the morning, along with some fresh fruits or veggies. You'll soon find yourself looking leaner, and you'll feel energized all morning long.

If you prefer a more traditional breakfast, eggs are a great way to start your day. Eggs are a highly nutritious food that is a good source of selenium, vitamin A, B vitamins, and certain minerals. In addition, almost all supermarkets now carry eggs that are enriched with the healthy long-chain omega 3 fatty acids, EPA and DHA. Most recent scientific studies show that regular egg consumption (seven per week) does not elevate your blood cholesterol level, nor does it increase your risk for heart disease. Rather, regular egg consumption increases the good HDL particles that remove cholesterol from your body while simultaneously reducing the artery-clogging small dense LDL particles that pro-mote heart disease. So go ahead and regularly include these healthful foods in your breakfast.

So Cal Omelet

Not just for breakfast, omelets are a great source of protein, any time of day. Try this vitamin-packed dish morning, noon, or night. SERVES 2

4 omega 3 eggs
1 tablespoon extra virgin olive oil
1 cup chopped spinach
1 teaspoon finely chopped fresh basil
Freshly ground black pepper
1 small avocado, thinly sliced

In a small mixing bowl, whisk eggs until frothy. Heat oil in a small skillet over medium flame. Add eggs. Using a rubber spatula, gently lift the edges of the omelet and allow uncooked egg to run off to the sides of the pan.

When eggs are almost set, layer the spinach over half of the omelet, sprinkle basil and pepper on the other half, and fold one half over the other. Reduce heat. Cover and simmer for one minute.

Cut in half, slide onto two plates, and garnish with sliced avocado.

Turkey Gobbler's Omelet

For turkey lovers, this recipe offers a delicious combination of meat and eggs to pack a powerful protein punch. SERVES 2

4 omega 3 eggs
1 tablespoon extra virgin olive oil
1 small red tomato, chopped
2 ounces Roasted Turkey Breast (page 90)
1 teaspoon chopped fresh dill

1 teaspoon dried tarragon
Freshly ground black pepper

In a small mixing bowl, whisk eggs until frothy. Heat oil in a small skillet over medium flame and add eggs. Using a rubber spatula, gently lift the edges of the omelet and allow uncooked eggs to run off to the side of the pan.

When eggs are almost set, place tomato and turkey on one side, sprinkle with dill and tarragon, and fold in half. Cover and simmer for one minute.

Cut in half and slide onto two plates. Season with fresh pepper to taste.

Fired-Up Steak and Eggs

For a healthy start to your day, enjoy this subtly sweet dish made from the freshest ingredients. SERVES 2

1 tablespoon extra virgin olive oil
1 green bell pepper, cut into strips
½ small onion, finely chopped
½ teaspoon chopped fresh basil
½ teaspoon dried rosemary
2 ounces Beef Tenderloin Roast, cut into strips (page 98)
2 omega 3 eggs, beaten
Freshly ground black pepper

Heat oil in cast iron skillet over medium flame. Add peppers, onions, basil, and rosemary and sauté for five minutes.

Layer with beef and continue to sauté one minute. Pour in eggs and stir all ingredients for two minutes.

Season with freshly ground black pepper to taste.

Eggciting Veggie Frittata

This simple veggie and egg dish, originating in Italy, is served open-faced, fresh from the oven. SERVES 2 OR 3

2 tablespoons extra virgin olive oil

1 red bell pepper, thinly sliced

1 small yellow onion, thinly sliced

1 garlic clove, minced

2 ounces white mushrooms, thinly sliced

4 large omega 3 eggs, beaten

Preheat oven to broil.

Heat oil in a cast iron skillet over medium flame. Add pepper, onion, and garlic. Sauté while stirring for about five minutes or until tender. Mix in mushrooms and continue cooking for five minutes, stirring occasionally. Pour in eggs and continue to stir occasionally for two additional minutes.

Place in oven and broil for three to four minutes until eggs are browned on top and firm to the touch.

Chick-Veggie Heaven

The versatile chicken lends so much of herself to our breakfast table. Forgo the eggs and enjoy the meat to get a scrumptious jump on your day. SERVES 2

2 tablespoons extra virgin olive oil

1 small yellow onion, chopped

1 garlic clove, minced

8 ounces fresh asparagus, chopped

1 large carrot, cut into matchsticks

8 ounces leftover Roasted Trussed Chicken, shredded (page 82)

8 ounces fresh, raw spinach

Juice from ½ lemon

In a cast iron skillet over medium flame, sauté onion and garlic for about five minutes or until tender. Add asparagus and carrot and continue to sauté for an additional five minutes. Mix in chicken and stir for one minute.

Fold in spinach, remove from heat, and cover. Spinach will wilt from the steam. Remove cover and drizzle mixture with fresh lemon juice.

Poached Eggs on Roasted Veggies

This unique combination lends flavor and variety to your breakfast table. SERVES 2

2 large omega 3 eggs

1 teaspoon freshly squeezed lemon juice

Leftover roasted veggies of your choice (see chapter 10 for options)

Fill a 9-inch saucepan with 1 inch of water. Add lemon juice and bring to a boil.

Crack eggs into a small dish. Lower the dish right next to surface of boiling water and let egg slide in. Cook eggs for three to four minutes and remove with a slotted spoon.

Place the eggs on top of the roasted vegetables.

Wild Salmon Delight

This omega 3 packed meal will start your day off with Paleo Diet perfection. SERVES 2

2 wild salmon fillets, 4–6 ounces each
1 tablespoon extra virgin olive oil
1 teaspoon finely chopped fresh dill
1 teaspoon ground paprika
½ teaspoon freshly ground black pepper
4 ounces white mushrooms, sliced
1 large red tomato, diced

Prepare a large saucepan with a steamer basket and 1 inch water. Bring to a boil. Reduce heat to simmer, place salmon in steamer, and cook for fifteen minutes.

Heat oil in a cast iron skillet over medium flame. Add dill, paprika, pepper, and mushrooms and sauté for five minutes. Mix in tomato and continue to sauté for an additional five minutes. Remove from heat.

Once salmon has finished cooking, remove from pan and top with mushroom and tomato mixture.

Breakfast in the Raw

Japanese cuisine frequently features raw fish, which is considered a delicacy. Brighten your day and sharpen your mind with this omega 3 eye-opener. SERVES 2

2 tablespoons coconut oil
2 cups spinach, torn into bite-sized pieces

2 ahi tuna sashimi, 4–6 ounces each, thinly sliced

1 cup mango or peach slices

½ cup blueberries

Warm coconut oil over low flame until liquid. Combine with spinach and toss well.

Arrange sashimi over spinach with mango or peach slices. Scatter with berries.

Morning Rainbow

Paleo Diet veterans have developed a taste for waking up to a freshly baked fish breakfast. This delicious dish will help you start your day with a splash. SERVES 2

2 wild-caught rainbow or other trout, 10–12 inches each

2 tablespoons extra virgin olive oil

½ sweet yellow onion, diced

2 tablespoons Chardonnay

1 teaspoon minced fresh dill

1 teaspoon paprika

Juice from ½ lemon

Preheat oven to 350 degrees. Clean trout thoroughly and place on a sheet of foil large enough to wrap entire fish.

In a small cast iron skillet, heat oil over medium flame. Add onion and sauté until tender, about five minutes. Remove from pan and place in a small mixing bowl.

Mix with wine, dill, paprika, and lemon juice. Stuff the trout with the onion mixture and wrap securely with foil. Bake for twenty minutes.

Spicy Breakfast Burrito

This south-of-the-border meal is a great alternative to a traditional tortilla-wrapped egg burrito. Using fresh crisp lettuce to wrap your breakfast provides you with a pure Paleo breakfast treat. SERVES 2

1 tablespoon extra virgin olive oil
½ sweet yellow onion, diced
1 garlic clove, pressed
½ red bell pepper, diced
1 teaspoon ground cumin
½ teaspoon cayenne pepper
½ cup cooked diced chicken, lean pork, or steak
3 large omega 3 eggs, beaten
½ teaspoon ground black pepper
2 large iceberg or romaine lettuce leaves

Heat olive oil in an 11-inch cast iron skillet over medium flame. Sauté onion and garlic until tender, about five minutes. Toss in bell pepper, cumin, cayenne pepper, and meat, mixing well for one minute.

Add beaten eggs and mix with a spatula until cooked thoroughly. Sprinkle with ground pepper. Wrap tightly in lettuce leaves.

Breakfast Express

Use your leftover broccoli and chicken to whip up this chopped breakfast entrée. This veggie-enhanced Waldorf salad makes the perfect start to your day. SERVES 2

2 cups steamed broccoli, cut into small pieces

8 ounces grilled chicken breast, diced

2 small red Delicious apples,cut into bite-sized pieces

1 ounce walnuts, chopped

½ cup halved grapes

1 large celery stalk, chopped

1 tablespoon flaxseed oil

1 teaspoon freshly squeezed lemon juice

Combine all ingredients in a medium bowl and toss well.

Shrimp Scramble

This shrimp and egg dish is a special treat to wake up your taste buds and power up your brain for the busy day ahead. Enjoy with a side of fresh melon, and you're off to a great start.

SERVES 2

1 tablespoon olive oil

¼ yellow onion, minced

4 omega 3 eggs

1 cup small cooked shrimp

1 teaspoon minced fresh dill

1 teaspoon dried basil

2 cooked artichoke hearts, fresh or canned (packed in water)

Heat oil in an 11-inch nonstick pan over medium flame. Add onion and sauté until tender, about five minutes.

In a medium bowl, beat eggs until frothy. Pour into pan with sautéed onions. Add shrimp, dill, and basil and mix thoroughly until eggs are wet but not completely cooked. Stir in artichoke hearts and finish cooking.

4

Paleo Snacks and Appetizers

Snack food and appetizers are very much a part of the Paleo Diet, and you should snack between meals whenever you get hungry. Our hunter-gatherer ancestors frequently snacked on some of the food they acquired while foraging and gathering. Just like our ancestors' snacks, yours should be nourishing and made from real foods. High-protein snack foods like beef jerky, dried salmon, peel-and-eat shrimp, or cold chicken breasts are a great way to satisfy your appetite, boost your metabolism, and help you lose weight. The key to Paleo snacks is to keep them simple so that you can bring them along with you to work or play. Resealable plastic bags or plastic food containers are a great way to keep your snacks fresh and accessible wherever you go. Here's a list of some simple snacks and appetizers that require minimal or no preparation time:

- Apples, plums, pears, peaches, apricots, grapes, strawberries, bananas, or any fresh fruit
- Dried apricots (unsulfured)
- Carrot and celery sticks dipped in guacamole
- Cherry or grape tomatoes
- Tomato quarters
- Jicama root cut into sticks
- Zucchini or squash rounds dipped in homemade salsa
- Avocado slices covered with lemon juice
- Hard-boiled eggs
- Homemade beef jerky
- Homemade dried salmon
- Cold London broil slices
- Cold turkey breast slices

- Cold peel-and-eat shrimp
- Cold chicken breast
- Cold pork tenderloin slices
- Steamed oysters
- Steamed clams
- Steamed mussels
- Cold crab legs
- Walnuts (limit to 4 ounces per day if you are trying to lose weight)

Appetizers are tidbits to linger over and nibble at for hours while having a drink or talking with friends. These are social foods, party foods, and celebration foods. These are dishes to inspire conversation and get the evening going. Seafood appetizers are very Paleo-friendly. They are neither too rich nor too filling, and they carry the quintessence of the ocean, being a little salty and pungent but also naturally fresh. They are high in protein and low in fat and are full of the healthy long-chain omega 3 fatty acids, EPA and DHA. What better way to start a party or celebration than with elegant platters of clams, oysters, lobster, shrimp, or crab legs? Garnish these delectable treats with raw fresh veggies such as scallions, cherry or grape tomatoes, radishes, or carrot curls, and your delicious appetizer will have breathtaking visual appeal as well.

Because Paleo appetizers focus on clean-flavored and nutritious raw ingredients, they make a wonderful light introduction to the more complex flavors that will follow in the main course. Good food can be accompanied by good wine on the Paleo Diet, so feel free to complement your appetizers and main dish with wine or whatever is the drink of your choice, including pure water.

Chili-Lime Shrimp

One of the best sources of protein and so easy to prepare, this shrimp appetizer is ready in just minutes. Serve hot or cold. SERVES 4

2 tablespoons extra virgin olive oil
1 garlic clove, minced
½ cup cherry tomatoes, sliced in half
1 pound medium shrimp
1 teaspoon paprika
2 tablespoons chopped cilantro
Juice from ½ lime
Cayenne pepper, to taste

Heat oil in a cast iron skillet over medium flame. Add garlic and sauté while stirring for one minute. Add tomatoes and continue cooking for two minutes. Toss in shrimp and continue stirring for two to three minutes. Shrimp is done when it becomes pink.

Turn off heat and toss with paprika and cilantro. Squeeze lime juice over the shrimp and sprinkle with cayenne pepper.

Mango-Strawberry Olé

We discovered this unique combination of sweet mango, strawberries, sour lime, and hot chili pepper on a hot summer night while vacationing in Mexico. SERVES 4

1 mango
4 large strawberries
Juice from ½ lime
Chili powder, to taste
4 cilantro sprigs, for garnish

Peel and slice mango into equal-sized strips. Wash and hull strawberries, then cut each lengthwise almost through but still in one piece. Arrange the mango in a fan shape, evenly distributed on each of four appetizer-sized plates. Place one strawberry, flat side down, on each plate. Drizzle fruit with lime juice. Sprinkle with chili powder. Top with cilantro sprig.

Asparagus Starter

A fresh light start to a special meal, this dish is sure to impress your dinner guests. SERVES 4

> 8 raw green asparagus spears (do not use baby asparagus as it is too thin)
>
> 8 pieces very thinly sliced Roast Turkey Breast (page 90)
>
> 2 tablespoons extra virgin olive oil
>
> 1 medium beefsteak tomato, thinly sliced
>
> ¼ red onion, thinly sliced
>
> Freshly ground black pepper, to taste

Fill a 2-quart pot halfway with water and insert a steamer basket. Bring to a boil. Place asparagus in basket and steam for five minutes. Remove from pot and plunge into ice water to stop the cooking process. Remove from water. Wrap one slice of turkey around each asparagus spear.

Heat 1 tablespoon oil in a cast iron skillet over medium flame. Place the spears in the pan, cover, and cook for one minute. Turn each wrapped asparagus over gently with tongs and continue cooking for one minute. The turkey will be nicely browned.

Place wrapped spears on paper towel to drain. Arrange spears on a serving platter and layer with tomato and onion slices. Drizzle with the remaining tablespoon of olive oil. Add freshly ground black pepper.

Pecan-Stuffed Figs

This Paleo hors d'oeuvre is a fast fix for last-minute guests. The addition of pecans to dried fruit is a perfect blend for this pre-meal snack. SERVES 4

8 fresh or dried figs
8 pecan halves

If using dried figs, place in bowl with 1 cup of water for thirty minutes to rehydrate.

Cut stems from figs and discard. Make a small slice across the top of each fig. Insert one pecan half into each.

Gazpacho

This vitamin-packed soup is traditionally served cold and pairs well with a fresh salad from your Paleo Diet menu (see chapter 9). SERVES 4

4 large beefsteak tomatoes, quartered
1 jalapeño pepper, diced
1 green bell pepper, diced
2 garlic cloves, crushed
1 small red onion, diced
1 small cucumber, peeled and diced
1 teaspoon freshly squeezed lime juice
2 tablespoons minced fresh cilantro
Freshly ground black pepper, to taste

Place tomatoes in food processor and puree until smooth.

Pour into medium bowl. Add peppers, garlic, onion, cucumber, and lime juice. Stir to combine. Sprinkle with cilantro and black pepper.

Beefed-Up Mini Wraps

This Paleo wrap is both simple to make and easy to take out for an on-the-go snack or to serve with any meal. SERVES 2

4 thin roast beef slices
1 small avocado, mashed
1 cup raw spinach, washed and coarsely chopped
1 small apple, washed and cut into 8 wedges
¼ teaspoon dried oregano
¼ teaspoon dried rosemary

Place beef slices on a smooth surface. Spread avocado over each piece of meat. Layer with spinach and apple wedges. Sprinkle with oregano and rosemary. Roll carefully to create wraps.

Grapes of Wrap

Serve these tasty wraps to your friends and family for a unique and savory start to a special Paleo meal. SERVES 4

8 ounces Roasted Trussed Chicken, shredded (page 82)
1 ounce raw walnuts, chopped
½ cup red grapes, chopped
½ teaspoon dried tarragon
½ teaspoon dried rosemary
4 Bibb or butter lettuce leaves
1 tablespoon cold-pressed flaxseed oil

In a medium bowl, combine chicken, walnuts, grapes, tarragon, and rosemary. Mix well.

Spoon an equal portion into each lettuce leaf. Drizzle with flaxseed oil. Roll lettuce leaves carefully and secure with toothpicks.

Melon Blankets

Take a break from the heat of the kitchen and wrap up your favorite melon with fresh lean turkey for a refreshing Paleo delight. SERVES 4

1 fresh cantaloupe, casaba, or honeydew melon, chilled
8 pieces of thinly sliced turkey breast, about 1 ounce
  each
Freshly ground black pepper

Remove seeds from center of melon and discard. Slice melon into eight equal wedges and remove rind.

Wrap one slice of turkey around each melon wedge and secure with toothpick. Dust with pepper.

Stuffed Tomatoes

These colorful little appetizers pair quite well with an evening barbecue or a holiday feast. Be sure to make plenty; they are bound to disappear in a hurry. SERVES 4

12 cherry tomatoes
¼ cup minced scallions
1 teaspoon dried basil
1 teaspoon dried oregano
1 tablespoon minced garlic
½ cup finely chopped spinach
1 tablespoon extra virgin olive oil
½ cup chopped fresh cilantro

Slice off stems and tops of each tomato. Using a small melon ball scoop, remove seeds from tomatoes, leaving them hollowed.

In a small bowl, combine scallions, basil, oregano, garlic, and spinach. Heat oil in a small skillet over medium flame. Add mixture and sauté for two minutes, stirring constantly.

Remove from heat and cool for ten minutes. Spoon into tomatoes and garnish with fresh cilantro.

Veggie Virtuoso

A veggie appetizer allows you to start a meal off right. Your taste buds will sing with delight over this Paleo-perfect appetizer. SERVES 4

> 1 red bell pepper, quartered
> 1 yellow bell pepper, quartered
> 1 small red onion, quartered
> 1 medium zucchini, sliced lengthwise
> 1 medium yellow squash, sliced lengthwise
> 2 tablespoons extra virgin olive oil
> 1 tablespoon dried oregano
> 1 tablespoon dried minced garlic
> 1 tablespoon minced fresh basil

Preheat oven to broil.

Combine vegetables in a bowl. Toss with oil, oregano, and garlic. Spread in a single layer on a rimmed baking sheet.

Broil thirty minutes, stirring at halfway point. Remove from oven and sprinkle with basil.

Tropical Deviled Eggs

Everyone loves deviled eggs. These versatile treats are the perfect snack, packed with protein to keep your energy level at its best throughout the day. SERVES 4

4 hard-boiled omega 3 eggs, halved
1 tablespoon coconut oil
1 tablespoon flaxseed oil
1 teaspoon ground ginger
Paprika, to taste

Remove yolks from eggs and place in a small mixing bowl. Add oils and ginger and mash together with a fork.

Using a small spoon, scoop the yolk mixture back into each egg half. Sprinkle with paprika.

Spicy Mixed Nuts

Making your own roasted nut mix allows you to be creative and confident that you are eating a Paleo-approved snack without the additives commonly found in the store-bought variety. MAKES 1½ CUPS

½ cup raw walnuts
½ cup raw brazil nuts
½ cup raw macadamia nuts
2 tablespoons extra virgin olive oil
1 teaspoon cayenne pepper
½ teaspoon ground nutmeg

Preheat oven to 400 degrees.

Combine nuts in a small bowl with oil, pepper, and nutmeg. Mix well. Place in a single layer on a rimmed baking sheet.

Roast nuts for fifteen minutes, stirring at the halfway point. Remove from oven and let cool.

Stuffed Shrooms

Mushrooms are a versatile and delicious addition to any Paleo cuisine. Try this delectable hors d'oeuvre as a prelude to your next dinner with friends. SERVES 4

12 medium mushrooms

1 tablespoon extra virgin olive oil

3 garlic cloves, pressed

½ cup diced shallots

1 tablespoon dried minced onion

¼ cup white wine

1 tablespoon dried basil

1 tablespoon dried oregano

1 tablespoon finely chopped fresh parsley

Remove stems from mushrooms and finely chop. Set aside. Heat olive oil in a saucepan over medium flame. Add garlic, shallots, and onion and sauté for two minutes while stirring. Pour in white wine and bring to a slight boil. Toss in chopped mushroom stems, basil, and oregano. Reduce heat to low and simmer for five minutes.

Remove from heat and drain off any excess liquid. Spoon into mushroom caps and top with fresh parsley.

Shrimp Skewers

Everyone loves a flavorful appetizer served on an easy-to-manage skewer. This omega 3–laden kebab will thrill the shrimp lovers at your festive dining table. SERVES 4

2 tablespoons extra virgin olive oil
3 garlic cloves, pressed
1 teaspoon paprika
1 teaspoon cayenne pepper
1 teaspoon dried dill
¼ cup white wine
20 medium shrimp, peeled
1 yellow bell pepper, seeded, cut in eighths
20 cherry tomatoes
Juice from 1 lime

Heat olive oil in a large pan over medium flame. Add garlic, paprika, cayenne, and dill. Sauté for one minute while stirring.

Reduce heat to low. Pour in white wine and simmer for two minutes. Add shrimp, cover and continue cooking for ten minutes. Shrimp are done when pink, with no gray coloring.

Place shrimp in a small colander and drain excess liquid. Spear shrimp, yellow pepper, and tomato, alternating each until skewer is full. Drizzle each kebab with fresh lime juice.

5

Paleo Poultry

Poultry should be a major component of your Paleo Diet menu, particularly if you can locate free-ranging birds that have access to grass, insects, and bugs. Check out Jo Robinson's Web site, www.eatwild.com, to find a producer near you. Chicken most often comes to mind in creating poultry dishes, but don't overlook turkey, duck, and goose, and even pheasant, quail, and dove fall into this appetizing category of meats. Grain-fed domestic ducks and geese are a lot like fatty feedlot-produced cattle: they are nutritionally inferior. Try to get the wild versions, if you can. The following three national suppliers specialize in wild poultry:

GAME SALES INTERNATIONAL

P.O. Box 7719
Loveland, CO 80537
(800) 729-2090
www.gamesalesinternational.com

POLARICA

105 Quint Street
San Francisco, CA 94124
(800) 426-3872
www.polarica.com

EXOTIC MEATS

1330 Capita Boulevard
Reno, NV 89502
(800) 444-5657
www.exoticmeatsandmore.com

Chicken and turkey are universally available, and because they are healthy and relatively inexpensive, make them a high-protein, low-fat staple in your diet. Chicken, with its moist white meat and savory dark meat, is a dinnertime delight that appeals to almost every diner, from a sophisticated gourmet to a finicky youngster.

Because it doesn't overpower other ingredients, chicken can be incorporated into an incredible diversity of dishes. How about stir-fried with veggies, tossed into a salad, grilled on a barbecue, whole roasted as an entrée, or made into a stew, a soup, or an omelet? The combinations are endless. Use your imagination in creating both simple and complex dishes—you can't go wrong with this bird.

You'll often see chickens labeled as "fryers," "broilers," and "roasters." Don't worry about frying a broiler or broiling a fryer. These terms simply refer to the size of the whole chicken, with fryers being the smallest, followed by broilers and roasters, which are typically the most expensive. A three-pound whole chicken feeds between two and four people, depending on appetites and accompanying foods.

Whole chicken costs the least on a per-pound basis, because the more it is butchered and cut, the more expensive it becomes. Boneless, skinless chicken breasts reduce your preparation time, but you'll pay extra. White meat is leaner and cooks more quickly, which makes it an excellent choice for quick sautés and grilling. Dark meat is less expensive, more flavorful, and great for stewing. If you can't get free-ranging, pasture-raised chicken, avoid the fattier pieces of factory-produced chickens, such as wings, thighs, and legs.

Turkey is traditional at Thanksgiving, but Paleo Dieters should keep it in mind all year round. Am I asking you to take half a day out of your busy schedules and roast a turkey with all the fixings? Absolutely not. Skinless turkey breast makes a good meal and is incredibly lean. Contrast its total fat (5 percent) to the fat of even a very lean venison roast (19 percent), and you can fully appreciate that this cut of turkey is one of the highest-protein sources (94 percent) I know of.

Ground turkey breast is also quite lean and makes a great burger. Be inventive; brown ground turkey breast in olive oil and throw it into a Mexican salad along with some Peach Salsa with a Punch (page 188), or fold it into a romaine lettuce wrap along with homemade Omega 3 Mayonnaise (page 196) and diced red onions.

Paleo Chicken in a Pot

The bouquet garni in this recipe makes this French dish both aromatic and flavorful. Serve with your favorite Paleo side dish and salad to complete your meal. SERVES 4

1 whole chicken, 2–3 pounds, quartered
Freshly ground black pepper
2 tablespoons olive oil
4 large carrots
1 bunch celery
4 small spring onions
4 fresh sage leaves
1 fresh rosemary sprig
1 bay leaf

Preheat oven to 300 degrees. Pepper chicken pieces thoroughly and set aside.

Pour olive oil into an ovenproof stockpot and heat over medium flame. Chop carrots, celery, and spring onions into 1-inch pieces. Sauté in olive oil for five minutes.

Add 1 quart of water. Place chicken in the pot. Using kitchen twine, tie together the sage leaves, rosemary, and bay leaf and place in the pot with the chicken. Cover and bake for one hour.

Remove the lid and turn oven setting to broil. Brown chicken for five minutes. Remove from oven and serve with broth and vegetables.

Homewood Chicken

Lean chicken breasts are the perfect Paleo choice to satisfy your protein requirements. Paired with fresh fruit, this meal is the Paleo version of comfort food. SERVES 4

4 chicken breasts, with bone and skin
Freshly ground black pepper, to taste
3 tablespoons extra virgin olive oil
1 fennel bulb, cored and sliced
1 pint cherry or grape tomatoes, washed and halved
½ cup coarsely chopped fresh basil
4 fresh basil leaves for garnish

Preheat oven to 425 degrees. Season chicken breasts thoroughly with freshly ground pepper.

Heat 2 tablespoons of the olive oil in a cast iron skillet over high flame. Place chicken in pan and sear each side for five minutes. Remove from pan and set aside.

Drain excess fat from pan and return pan to burner, adding fennel, tomatoes, and the remaining tablespoon of olive oil. Place chicken in pan and sprinkle with chopped basil.

Cover with foil and bake for thirty minutes. Change oven setting to broil. Remove foil and set under broiler for five minutes.

Remove from oven and tent with foil. After five minutes, garnish each chicken breast with fresh basil leaves.

Coconut-Cashew Chicken

Prepared with all-natural ingredients, the flavors of this simple dish will have your taste buds begging for more. Make a batch of curry ahead of time, and you can have this recipe whipped up in minutes. SERVES 4

4 skinless, boneless chicken breasts, pounded thin
with meat tenderizer tool
1 cup Coconut Curry (page 185)
¼ cup chopped roasted cashews

Combine chicken and curry and marinate in the refrigerator for at least two hours. Remove from refrigerator thirty minutes before cooking.

Preheat oven to broil. Place chicken on wire rack and cook for twenty minutes, turning at the halfway point.

Remove from oven and scatter with cashews.

Roasted Trussed Chicken

Sometimes the simplest recipes with the fewest ingredients make the tastiest meals. This dish can be enjoyed as a main course or used as an addition to soup or salad. SERVES 4

1 whole chicken, 2–3 pounds
1 tablespoon extra virgin olive oil
1 teaspoon paprika
Freshly ground black pepper

Preheat oven to 425 degrees. Set chicken on a wire roasting rack, breast side up. Place a 2-foot piece of kitchen twine under the body of the chicken, making sure to leave an even length on each side. Tuck the drumsticks tightly together to cover the open cavity at the bottom of the chicken and secure with the twine; tuck the wings under the legs and crisscross the twine to secure. Turn the bird to the side to tie tightly, then return it to breast facing up. Rub the olive oil and paprika over the breast, legs, and wings of the bird. Sprinkle with freshly ground black pepper.

Cook for one hour and fifteen minutes. Remove from oven, tent with foil, and set aside for ten minutes. Remove from wire roasting rack to carve.

Greek Chicken Breast Kebabs

Everyone loves a kebab. This easy-to-prepare and fun-to-eat dish makes a festive presentation and will impress your guests. Be sure to make plenty as there will be many requests for seconds. SERVES 4

1 tablespoon freshly squeezed lemon juice

2 teaspoons dried oregano

1 tablespoon olive oil

1 garlic clove, crushed

4 6-ounce chicken cutlets, cut into 1-inch cubes

8 skewers, wooden or metal

If using wooden skewers, soak in water for one hour.

Combine lemon juice with oregano, oil, and garlic in a small jar and shake well. Pour over chicken and mix well. Cover and refrigerate for at least two hours.

Thread chicken onto skewers. Grill or broil at medium heat for twenty minutes, turning at the halfway point.

Paleo Chicken Saltimbocca

Lean sliced turkey (in place of prosciutto and provolone) is the secret to keeping this classic Italian dish Paleo-friendly. The combination of two poultry staples is a marriage made in heaven. SERVES 4

4 chicken breasts, boneless and skinless, pounded thin
   with meat tenderizer tool
Freshly ground black pepper, to taste
2 tablespoons extra virgin olive oil
4 fresh sage leaves
4 thin slices of natural, organic Roasted Turkey Breast
   (page 90)

Preheat oven to 425 degrees. Season chicken breasts thoroughly with black pepper and set aside.

Heat oil in a cast iron skillet over medium flame. Place sage leaves in skillet and cook for thirty seconds on each side. Remove and drain on a paper towel.

Press one slice of turkey onto each chicken breast. Cook chicken breast for four minutes on turkey side, then turn with tongs and cook on other side.

Remove chicken from pan and place in baking dish. Press one sage leaf on top of each piece of cooked chicken. Bake for ten minutes.

Colorado Chicken

Using skin-on, bone-in chicken breast leads to moist and tender meat. Follow these simple steps to enjoy a flavorful treat.

SERVES 4

2 tablespoons extra virgin olive oil

4 bone-in, skin on chicken breasts

Freshly ground black pepper

8 ounces white mushrooms, sliced

1 medium shallot, diced

1 small tomato, diced

2 cups Chicken Broth (page 193)

1 tablespoon chopped fresh tarragon

1 tablespoon chopped fresh parsley

Preheat oven to 425 degrees.

Heat oil in a cast iron skillet over medium flame. Sprinkle chicken breasts with black pepper and place in pan. Cover and cook for five minutes on each side.

Remove chicken and set aside. Place mushrooms in pan and cook, stirring occasionally, for ten minutes. Add shallots and continue stirring for two additional minutes.

Add tomatoes and broth. Bring to a boil, then reduce heat and simmer for five minutes. Return chicken to pan, cover, and bake for twenty minutes. Remove from oven and sprinkle with tarragon and parsley.

Chicken Marsala

This family-favorite chicken dish will please young and old alike. The mellow flavors of mushrooms and Marsala wine combine to make this a moist and succulent dish. SERVES 4

2 tablespoons extra virgin olive oil
4 boneless and skinless chicken breasts, 6 ounces each, pounded with meat tenderizer tool
1 cup chopped assorted wild mushrooms
1 shallot, chopped
½ cup Marsala wine
½ cup Chicken Broth (page 193)
½ teaspoon dried oregano

Heat oil in a cast iron skillet over medium flame. Add chicken breasts and cook ten minutes, turning at halfway point. Remove from pan and tent with foil.

Add mushrooms to pan and cook for five minutes, stirring occasionally. Stir in shallot and cook for one additional minute. Pour in wine and broth and bring to a boil.

Reduce heat and simmer over low flame for twenty minutes. Use a spatula to scrape browned bits from the surface of the pan and mix with liquid.

Place chicken back in skillet and cook for five minutes. Sprinkle with oregano.

Chicken Braised with Celery

You will enjoy this easy-to-prepare, delicious, and healthy treat. The addition of Paleo-friendly broth makes this a low-sodium meal for any time of day. SERVES 4

2 tablespoons extra virgin olive oil

4 bone-in, skin-on chicken breasts

1 medium shallot, thinly sliced

12 celery stalks, sliced in half lengthwise and widthwise

4 large carrots, peeled and sliced in half lengthwise and widthwise

½ cup Chicken Broth (page 193)

½ cup dry white wine

Preheat oven to 400 degrees.

Heat oil in a cast iron skillet over medium flame. Add chicken and cook, skin side down, for five minutes. Turn chicken over and continue cooking for five minutes. Remove from pan and tent with foil.

Add shallot to pan and cook for one minute. Add celery and carrots and cook without stirring for two minutes. Turn pieces to brown evenly and cook for two additional minutes.

Place chicken back in skillet, skin side down. Pour in broth and wine. Cook for twenty minutes, turning at halfway point.

Change oven setting to broil and bake chicken for three minutes to brown the skin. Remove from oven and cool for five minutes.

Paleo Turkey Burgers

This recipe is worth doubling to have extra on hand. Turkey burgers are perfect for a midday snack, crumbled up into an omelet for a bit of extra protein, or frozen for use later in the week. SERVES 6

2 pounds lean ground turkey breast

1 egg

1 tablespoon extra virgin olive oil

1 small shallot, chopped

1 garlic clove, minced

1 teaspoon freshly ground black pepper

1 teaspoon dried oregano

1 medium beefsteak tomato, sliced

½ small red onion, sliced into four ¼-inch slices

1 small head Bibb or butter lettuce

Preheat oven to broil. Combine turkey with egg, oil, shallot, and garlic. Mix well and shape into six patties. Season with pepper and oregano.

Broil patties for five minutes on each side. Remove from oven and serve topped with tomato and onion. Place inside lettuce, and top with your favorite Paleo condiments (see chapter 11).

Paleo Turkey Fajitas

Fajitas have become a favorite food for many families. The Paleo-perfect ingredients in this recipe allow you to enjoy the flavors of Mexico in a healthy way. SERVES 4

4 tablespoons extra virgin olive oil
2 garlic cloves, crushed
2 tablespoons freshly squeezed lime juice
1 teaspoon chili powder
1 teaspoon ground cumin
1½ pounds turkey cutlets, cut into ½-inch strips
1 small yellow onion, cut into 8 wedges
1 red bell pepper, cut into ½-inch strips
1 yellow bell pepper, cut into ½-inch strips
¼ cup chopped cilantro
1 small bunch scallions, thinly sliced
Holy Guacamole (page 190)

Combine 2 tablespoons of the oil with the garlic, lime, chili powder, and cumin in a large bowl. Add turkey and mix well. Cover and refrigerate for at least two hours. Remove from refrigerator thirty minutes before cooking.

Heat the remaining 2 tablespoons of olive oil in a cast iron skillet over medium flame. Add onion and peppers and cook for ten minutes, stirring occasionally. Toss in turkey and cook for ten minutes, stirring continuously.

Scatter with cilantro and sliced scallions. Serve topped with guacamole.

Roasted Turkey Breast

Try preparing this family favorite for your next holiday feast. Lean meat infused with savory spices makes this meal healthy and delicious. SERVES 4

4 tablespoons cold-pressed olive oil
1 tablespoon chopped rosemary
1 tablespoon chopped sage
1 garlic clove, crushed
1 bone-in, skin-on turkey breast, 2–3 pounds

Preheat oven to 325 degrees.

Combine oil with rosemary, sage, and garlic. Rub into turkey flesh, both under and on the skin. Place turkey breast in a roasting pan and cover with foil. Cook for one hour.

Remove from oven and let rest for five minutes before carving.

Cajun Blackened Turkey Cutlets

If Southern cooking is your pleasure, you will find this dish a great way to satisfy both your cravings and your protein needs. Feel free to go back for seconds with this healthy and flavorful meal. SERVES 4

1 teaspoon paprika
1 teaspoon onion powder
1 teaspoon garlic powder
1 teaspoon oregano
2 teaspoons cayenne pepper
2 teaspoons white pepper
4 6-ounce turkey cutlets, pounded thin with meat
    tenderizer tool
2 tablespoons extra virgin olive oil

Combine paprika, onion powder, garlic powder, oregano, and peppers. Place spice mixture in a large plastic bag and add turkey. Close bag and shake well to thoroughly coat turkey.

Heat oil in a cast iron skillet over high flame. Add turkey and cook for ten minutes, turning at the halfway point. Remove from skillet and tent with foil for five minutes.

Pan-Seared Duck Breast

Wild duck can be a little more difficult to find than chicken or turkey, but it is worth the search. Be sure you are getting all natural, healthy meat. Try your local health-food store and carefully trim all visible fat from the meat before serving to ensure the leanest presentation. SERVES 4

4 duck breasts, skin removed
2 tablespoons extra virgin olive oil
1 star anise, crushed
1 teaspoon freshly grated ginger root
2 garlic cloves, crushed
1 large carrot, julienned
2 portobello mushrooms, chopped
2 small plums, quartered
¼ cup chopped cilantro

Slice duck into thin strips and set aside.

Heat oil in a cast iron skillet over medium flame. Add star anise, ginger, and garlic. Sauté for one minute before adding carrot and mushrooms. Continue to sauté for five minutes, stirring occasionally.

Place duck slices into skillet and sauté for an additional ten minutes. Toss in plums and cilantro and stir ingredients for one minute.

Ground Duck Burgers with Rosemary

For a twist on the traditional beef burger, try this recipe at your next get-together. Your guests will be pleasantly surprised at the juicy flavors that make this dish the perfect Paleo treat.
SERVES 4

4 duck breasts, skin removed
1 egg
1 tablespoon chopped rosemary
1 teaspoon garlic powder
Freshly ground black pepper
1 small bunch scallions, chopped
1 heirloom tomato, thickly sliced
1 small head Bibb or butter lettuce

Preheat oven to broil or set grill to medium flame.

Remove skin from duck breasts, trim visible fat, and slice breasts into bite-sized pieces. Put all meat through a grinder and place in a large mixing bowl.

Combine duck meat with egg, rosemary, and garlic powder. Mix well and shape into four patties. Season with freshly ground pepper to taste.

Broil burgers for twenty minutes, flipping them at the halfway point. Garnish with scallions and tomato. Serve with a lettuce-leaf "bun," and top with your favorite Paleo condiments (see chapter 11).

Herbed Roasted Pheasant

Our Paleo ancestors frequently dined on wild birds and most likely found them to be easy to prepare, with no leftovers to store. Your family will enjoy this succulent dish prepared with the freshest ingredients. SERVES 4

2 tablespoons extra virgin olive oil

1 tablespoon minced rosemary

1 tablespoon minced thyme

1 tablespoon minced sage

1 pheasant, 2–3 pounds

2 large carrots, chopped into large pieces

4 celery stalks, chopped into large pieces

1 small yellow onion, chopped into large pieces

Chicken Broth (page 193)

Preheat oven to 350 degrees.

Combine oil with rosemary, thyme, and sage and brush over entire bird. Mix carrots, celery, and onion and stuff inside cavity of pheasant.

Place bird on wire rack in roasting pan. Pour chicken broth into bottom of pan. Roast for approximately thirty minutes. Remove from oven and tent with foil for ten minutes before carving.

6

Paleo Beef, Pork, and Lamb

Many years ago, B.C. (before children), when Lorrie and I were first married and just beginning our lifelong journey with what has become known as the Paleo Diet, we had a delightful summer feast of grilled London broil, steamed artichokes, spinach salad, a glass of merlot, and a bowl of fresh blackberries for dessert. What better way to enjoy an evening at Lake Tahoe? In those early days, I felt slightly guilty because I had just consumed a great big slab of delicious, rare beef.

Before the Paleo Diet, my view of a healthy diet was one devoid of red meat, primarily plant-based, and loaded with whole grains, brown rice, beans, and low-fat dairy products. I had eaten in this manner for nearly twenty years, and I now know that my health and fitness suffered for it. If I had only listened to my body carefully, I would have realized why I felt so bad after my breakfast bowl of brown rice, skim milk, and sliced bananas. By 10 am, I was ravished and jittery, so I usually ate some high-carb snack just to make it until lunch.

In those days I didn't realize that my so-called healthy breakfast had just shot my blood sugar and insulin levels sky-high, and they were only to plummet a few hours later. As lean meat, eggs, and fish became my breakfast staples, along with some fresh fruit, my energy level stabilized throughout the morning, and I felt alert and fit. After I permanently adopted this lifelong way of eating, my chronic lower back pain disappeared, as did my semiannual upper respiratory illnesses. My overall health blossomed, and so will yours when you become a Paleo Dieter. Rest assured, there is absolutely no need to feel guilty about eating a big slab of lean red meat.

In this chapter, we encourage you to get lean beef, lamb, and pork back into your diet if you haven't already done so. Meat is the largest contributor of readily available iron and zinc and a major supplier of omega 3 fatty acids, particularly if your meat is grass-produced. Meat is one of the best sources of vitamin B_{12} and easily absorbable vitamin B_6.

Believe it or not, lean meats such as sirloin steak, pork loin, and flank steak will lower your total blood cholesterol and triglyceride levels while simultaneously increasing HDL (the good cholesterol), especially when they are part of a low-glycemic-load diet—and that is exactly what you will be eating with all of the delicious recipes in *The Paleo Diet Cookbook*.

Beef Tenderloin Roast

Who doesn't love a nice beef filet when dining with family and friends? Buy a roast that has been tied, following the simple tips below to ensure even cooking. Using grass-fed beef makes this dish pure Paleo. SERVES 4

1 2-pound filet mignon roast, tied
2 tablespoons extra virgin olive oil
1 cup chopped cremini mushrooms
1 garlic clove
1 small shallot
¼ cup chopped fresh parsley
4 tablespoons cold-pressed flaxseed oil
3 or 4 large kale leaves

Remove roast from refrigerator thirty minutes prior to cooking. Preheat oven to 325 degrees.

Heat olive oil in a cast iron skillet over medium flame. Add mushrooms and sauté until tender, for five to seven minutes. Remove mushrooms from skillet and set aside.

Return the skillet to high heat and sear the roast for three minutes on each side, until evenly browned. Transfer the roast to a roasting pan and place in oven. While cooking, check the internal temperature of the meat with a meat thermometer: 120 degrees for rare, 130 degrees for medium rare, 140 degrees for medium, and 160 degrees for well-done. Remove from oven and tent with foil.

Combine the garlic, shallot, parsley, and flaxseed oil in a small food processor and grind till well combined. Snip the string from the beef. Slice and drizzle with sauce. Serve over kale leaves.

Beef Stew with Vegetables

The sweet aroma of stewing meat, mixed with the freshest ingredients, will have your mouth watering for more. Go ahead and indulge. This recipe is Paleo-perfect for warming up a cold winter's night. SERVES 4

4 tablespoons extra virgin olive oil

2 pounds chuck steak, cut into cubes

1 medium yellow onion, chopped

2 garlic cloves, crushed

4 large carrots, peeled and cut into 1-inch pieces

4 celery stalks, cut into 1-inch pieces

1 small butternut squash, peeled, seeded, and cut into 1-inch cubes

2 cups Chicken Broth (page 193)

1 bay leaf

1 sprig fresh rosemary

1 teaspoon dried oregano

Freshly ground black pepper, to taste

Heat 2 tablespoons of the oil in a cast iron skillet over medium flame. Add meat to skillet and brown evenly on all sides, for approximately twelve minutes. Remove from skillet.

Add the remaining 2 tablespoons of oil, onion, and garlic to pan. Sauté for five minutes. Toss in carrots, celery, and squash and sauté for five additional minutes.

Return beef to skillet. Pour in broth. Bring to a boil, then cover and reduce heat to low. Add bay leaf, rosemary, and oregano. Cover and simmer for thirty minutes. Sprinkle with black pepper.

Carne Asada

Have a fiesta today and celebrate the spicy traditions of Mexico. This dish will have you dreaming of the sizzling beaches of Cancun. SERVES 4

1 jalapeño pepper
1 teaspoon ground cumin
2 tablespoons minced fresh cilantro
1 tablespoon freshly squeezed lime juice
2 tablespoons extra virgin olive oil
2 pounds flank steak, pounded thin with meat tenderizer tool

Combine pepper, cumin, cilantro, lime juice, and oil in a small container. Put steak in a large flat dish and pour mixture evenly over top. Marinate in refrigerator for at least two hours.

Preheat oven to broil or ignite the grill. Broil or grill for ten minutes, turning at the halfway point. Remove from heat and tent with foil for five minutes.

Paleo Tamales in Banana Leaves

We have grown to love the spicy flavors in south-of-the-border foods. This tasty recipe is in keeping with tradition while using only Paleo-approved ingredients. Olé! SERVES 4

1 tablespoon extra virgin olive oil

1 small yellow onion, diced

1 cup diced button mushrooms

1 cup chayote squash, diced (if unavailable, use zucchini or yellow squash)

1 pound lean ground beef

1 tablespoon freshly ground flaxseed meal

1 teaspoon chili powder

2 scallions, chopped

½ teaspoon freshly ground pepper

8 fresh banana leaves, soaked in water for one hour

Cut each banana leaf into an 8 × 10-inch square and a 12-inch strip.

Heat oil in a skillet over medium flame. Add onion and sauté for five minutes. Toss in mushrooms and squash. Continue to sauté for five minutes. Add beef, stirring for five minutes or until thoroughly browned. Remove from heat.

Stir in flaxseed meal, chili powder, and scallions. Arrange equal portions in the centers of the banana leaf squares. Fold top and bottom of each square in, and then roll each tamale into a rectangular shape. Tie with 12-inch banana leaf strips.

Fill a 4-quart pot with 1 inch of water. Insert steamer basket and bring to boil. Place tamales in basket and cover. Reduce heat to low and simmer for one hour.

Beef Bourguignon

This popular French recipe is packed with flavorful ingredients to please your palate. Enjoy with a salad and fresh fruit for the ultimate Paleo meal. SERVES 4

2 tablespoons extra virgin olive oil

2 pounds chuck steak, cut into cubes

8 ounces white pearl onions

2 garlic cloves, crushed

2 large carrots, cut into 1-inch pieces

2 large celery stalks, cut into 1-inch pieces

1 cup chanterelle mushrooms

2 large plum tomatoes, seeded and chopped

2 cups dry red wine

2 cups Chicken Broth (page 193)

1 bay leaf

1 sprig rosemary

1 sprig thyme

Heat 1 tablespoon of the oil in a large stockpot over medium flame. Add beef in a single layer (working in stages, if necessary) and cook for two minutes on each side. Remove from skillet.

Add the remaining tablespoon of olive oil and pearl onions. Sauté for five minutes. Add garlic, carrots, celery, and mushrooms. Cook for five minutes, stirring occasionally. Toss in tomatoes and cook two additional minutes. Pour in wine and broth. Bring to a boil.

Tie bay leaf, rosemary, and thyme together with kitchen twine to make a bouquet garni. Place meat and bouquet garni inside pot with vegetables, reduce heat to low, and cover. Simmer for two and a half to three hours. Remove bouquet garni.

Paleo Fajita Stir-Fry

This dish is an interesting fusion approach to stir-fry. Traditional Latin spices combined with the optional kick of dark Jamaican rum make an interesting marriage of flavors. SERVES 4

- 2 pounds skirt steak, pounded thin with meat tenderizer tool and cut into 1-inch strips
- 4 tablespoons extra virgin olive oil
- 2 garlic cloves, crushed
- 2 tablespoons freshly squeezed lime juice
- 1 teaspoon chili powder
- 1 teaspoon ground cumin
- 1 small yellow onion, cut into thin wedges
- 1 red bell pepper, cut into ¼-inch strips
- 1 yellow bell pepper, cut into ¼-inch strips
- 1 medium plum tomato, diced
- 2 tablespoons dark rum (optional)
- ¼ cup chopped fresh cilantro

Place meat in bottom of a glass dish. Combine 2 tablespoons of the oil with garlic, lime juice, chili powder, and cumin in a jar and shake well. Pour over meat and marinate at least two hours in the refrigerator.

Heat the remaining 2 tablespoons of oil in a skillet over medium flame. Add meat strips in a single layer and cook without stirring for one minute. Turn meat and continue cooking for one minute. Add onion and peppers and continue to cook for four minutes, stirring occasionally.

Combine tomato and rum in a small bowl. Stir with a fork and pour into skillet. Cook for one minute. Sprinkle with cilantro. Remove from heat and cool for three minutes.

Veal Scaloppine

Quick and simple to prepare, this recipe is perfect for a busy Paleo Dieter. SERVES 4

2 tablespoons extra virgin olive oil

4 veal cutlets, 4–6 ounces each, pounded thin with meat tenderizer tool

1 cup sliced cremini mushrooms

1 medium shallot, thinly sliced

1 cup Chicken Broth (page 193)

¼ cup minced fresh parsley

Heat 1 tablespoon of the olive oil in a cast iron skillet over medium flame. Add veal cutlets and cook for four minutes, turning at the halfway point. Remove from skillet and place on paper towels to drain.

Add mushrooms and shallot to skillet with the remaining tablespoon of olive oil and sauté for five minutes. Pour in broth. Scrape browned bits from bottom of skillet. Bring to a boil and stir for one minute.

Reduce heat to medium and add veal. Cook for one minute, just long enough to heat veal. Stir in parsley.

Braised Pork Shoulder

Serve this meal to family and friends and you will have given them the gift of a delicious and nutritious dining experience. What better way to show your love? SERVES 4

1 tablespoon extra virgin olive oil

1 2-pound pork shoulder roast

1 large yellow onion, chopped

2 medium shallots, thinly sliced

4 celery stalks, cut in half lengthwise, then into
    2-inch pieces

1 large leek, root and top green portion removed,
    cut into 1-inch rounds

½ cup Chicken Broth (page 193)

½ cup white wine

Freshly ground white pepper

Heat oil in a large stockpot over medium flame. Add pork shoulder and cook for eight minutes, browning evenly on all sides. Remove and set aside.

Add onion to pot and cook for five minutes. Stir in shallots and cook for one minute longer. Place celery and leek in pot and cook for four minutes, turning at the halfway point. Pour in broth and wine. Return pork to pot. Cook for two and a half hours, basting every thirty minutes. Sprinkle with pepper to taste.

Apricot-Stuffed Pork Tenderloin

The unique combination of fruit and spices in this meat dish will wake up your taste buds and satisfy your protein needs for the day. SERVES 4

1½–2 pounds pork tenderloin, cut in half lengthwise
2 tablespoons extra virgin olive oil
½ cup chopped white mushrooms
1 medium shallot, diced
2 garlic cloves, crushed
½ cup dried unsulfured apricots, chopped and soaked
   in water for thirty minutes
¼ cup dry white wine
Freshly ground white pepper, to taste

Remove pork from refrigerator thirty minutes prior to cooking. Preheat oven to 350 degrees.

Heat 1 tablespoon of the oil in a cast iron skillet over medium flame. Add mushrooms and sauté for five minutes. Toss in shallot and garlic and continue to sauté for two minutes. Add apricots and wine. Scrape browned bits off bottom of skillet and stir. Bring to a quick boil, and then reduce heat to low. Simmer for five minutes, or until liquid has evaporated. Remove from heat.

Cool mixture for five minutes, then place in a food processor and puree until smooth. Spread mixture down the middle of one of the loin halves. Place the other half on top and tie every 2 inches with kitchen twine.

Add the remaining tablespoon of olive oil to a roasting pan. Place tied loin in pan and bake for fifteen minutes. Turn loin over and bake for an additional fifteen minutes. Remove from oven and tent with foil. Let rest for ten minutes.

Paleo Posole

A pork posole, or thick soup, typically features hominy grits, but this Paleo recipe uses squash instead. You will find this dish tasty, light, and healthy. SERVES 4

1½ pounds pork shoulder

1 small yellow onion, chopped

4 garlic cloves, minced

1 teaspoon ground cumin

1 teaspoon oregano

1 teaspoon red pepper flakes

2 tablespoons extra virgin olive oil

2 cups 1-inch cubes peeled acorn squash

1 small jalapeño pepper, minced

2 tablespoons chopped fresh cilantro

Place pork shoulder in a large stockpot. Add 3 cups of water, onion, garlic, cumin, oregano, and red pepper. Bring to a boil and cover. Reduce heat to low and simmer for one hour. Remove from heat.

Take pork shoulder from pot and set aside. Pour liquid and onions into a large bowl. Heat olive oil in stockpot over medium flame. Add squash and cook for five minutes, stirring occasionally for even browning.

Return pork, liquid, and spice mixture to pot. Add jalapeño, bring to a boil, and cover. Reduce heat to low and simmer for ninety minutes. Stir in fresh cilantro. The dish is ready when the meat falls off the bone easily.

Perfect Pot Roast

Slow cooking is the secret to the tenderness of this hearty dish. The resulting flavorful meal is definitely worth the wait.

SERVES 4

1 teaspoon ground cumin

1 teaspoon chili powder

1 teaspoon oregano

1 teaspoon cayenne pepper

1 teaspoon paprika

1 2-pound chuck roast

2 tablespoons extra virgin olive oil

4 large celery stalks, cut into 2-inch pieces

4 large carrots, cut into 2-inch pieces

1 large white onion, cut into 8 wedges

1 cup Chicken Broth (page 193)

1 cup Marsala wine

Combine cumin, chili powder, oregano, cayenne, and paprika in a small bowl. Evenly coat roast with spices.

In a large stockpot, heat oil over medium flame. Brown roast for eight minutes, turning occasionally to ensure even browning. Add celery, carrots, and onions. Sauté for five minutes. Pour in broth and wine. Bring to a boil.

Cover, reduce heat, and simmer for two to two and a half hours, stirring occasionally.

Ike's Moussaka

Who needs béchamel? With a blend of eggplant, tomato, lamb, and spices, this dish is highly flavorful and very tasty in its own right. SERVES 4

2 large eggplants

1 tablespoon extra virgin olive oil

1 small onion, diced

2 large plum tomatoes, seeded and chopped

2 garlic cloves, crushed

2 pounds ground lamb

1 teaspoon cinnamon

1 teaspoon ground nutmeg

Freshly ground black pepper, to taste

2 tablespoons chopped parsley

Preheat oven to broil. Cut eggplants in half and place cut sides down in a glass baking dish with 1 inch of water. Bake for thirty minutes, flipping halfway through. The eggplant is done when the skin is easily pierced with a fork.

Remove eggplant from oven and cool for ten minutes, cut sides up. Scoop flesh out, being careful not to tear the skins. Place flesh in a bowl and mash with a fork. Set aside.

Preheat oven to 350 degrees. Heat oil in a cast iron skillet over medium flame. Add onion and sauté for five minutes. Toss in tomatoes and continue cooking for two minutes. Add garlic and cook for one additional minute. Place ground lamb in skillet and sauté for five minutes, or until thoroughly browned. Sprinkle in cinnamon, nutmeg, and pepper to taste. Stir in mashed eggplant. Remove from heat and add parsley.

(continued)

Ike's Moussaka (continued)

Place cooled eggplant skins in a charlotte pan with skin edges hanging over the top. Spoon lamb mixture into eggplant skins, folding edges of eggplant over the top. Bake for one hour. Remove from oven and cool for ten minutes.

Paleo Bison, Game Meat, and Jerky

Except for wild game, grass- or pasture-produced meat is one of the healthiest foods you can eat. Free-ranging, grass-fed meats, poultry, and eggs are superior in every nutritional respect when compared to feedlot-produced, grain-fed, or factory-produced meats. Livestock allowed to graze naturally in pastures and fields yield leaner meat, which contains more healthful omega 3 fatty acids, less omega 6 fatty acids, and less saturated fat than their grain-fed, factory-produced counterparts. Lorrie and I buy half sides of grass-fed beef and bison from local producers here in Colorado. We love it—it tastes better than feedlot-produced meat and we know it is much healthier for us and our children. Also, by skipping the middleman and buying directly from the producer, we get our meat at a reduced price.

If you don't have the luxury of buying directly from a local producer, how do you know if your hard-earned bucks are really buying pasture-produced meat? You can tell by the color of the fat. Grass-fed meats have fat that is slightly orange, whereas the fat of feedlot-produced meat is bright white. Why is this? Grass contains a nutrient called beta-carotene, which is also found in carrots and cantaloupe and gives them their distinctive orange colors. When animals eat beta-carotene-containing grass, it turns their fat slightly orange.

As I mentioned earlier, it takes a little sleuthing to find grass-fed meats from reliable sources, simply because compared to massive agribusiness feedlots, farms and ranches that raise animals in pastures remain a small cottage industry. Many of the upscale health-oriented supermarkets, such as Whole Foods, carry grass-fed meats. Much of the meat produced in countries like Australia, New Zealand, and Argentina is raised in pastures rather than in feedlots.

If you have abandoned lamb chops because you thought they were too fatty, check out the Australian or New Zealand chops made from grass-fed lambs. They are much leaner than their U.S. counterparts and are good sources of omega 3 fatty acids. Jo Robinson's Web site, Eat Wild (www.eatwild.com), is unsurpassed for locating farmers and ranchers in your vicinity who specialize in raising grass-fed animals.

Meat from grass-fed animals will awaken your taste buds with a magnificent flavor that is missing from feedlot-produced meats. Now that I have had the luxury of eating meat from grass-fed animals, the meat of grain-fed animals tastes bland and lackluster. There is no need for elaborate sauces, salt, or overpowering spices with meat from grass-fed animals; its own flavor will captivate you.

If you have never tasted game, make sure that your first experience is a good one. When properly harvested, cleaned, and cooked, game has rich, wonderful flavors with overtones of wild herbs and berries that simply cannot be duplicated with commercial meats. Some people are reluctant to eat wild meats because they may taste too "gamy." This quality typically comes from animals that were improperly dressed or incorrectly cooked. If you are trying game meat for the first time, I recommend bison or elk cooked medium rare so as not to dry it out. Both have a flavor that is similar to beef, but richer and more savory.

One of my favorite Paleo treats is jerky, but not the kind of jerky you find at convenience stores or supermarkets. Because commercial jerky is laced with salt, sugar, nitrites, and other non-Paleo additives, you will have to make your own jerky. This is not an insurmountable task; my twelve-year-old does it all the time. The only item that you will need is a small food dehydrator, which can be purchased for forty to sixty dollars from almost any commercial outlet offering small appliances. You can try our favorite Paleo jerky recipe in this chapter or experiment with your own combinations of herbs and spices. Jerky is a high-protein, low-fat food that comes in handy all day long to satisfy your appetite.

Bison-Stuffed Bell Peppers

These are *not* your mom's stuffed peppers. Gone are the bread crumbs, ketchup, salt, and cheese. This recipe offers a modern lean and mean version sure to satisfy your Paleo appetite.
SERVES 4

4 bell peppers, assorted colors
1 tablespoon extra virgin olive oil
1 pound ground bison
1 omega 3 egg
1 scallion, thinly sliced
Garlic powder, to taste
Cayenne pepper, to taste

Preheat oven to 350 degrees. Cut tops from peppers and remove seeds. Rub the outer surface of each pepper with oil. Place peppers, cut sides up, in an oiled baking dish.

Combine ground bison with egg in a medium bowl. Using your hands, mix well. Add scallion and mix again. Sprinkle with garlic powder and cayenne pepper.

Stuff peppers with equal portions of meat mixture. Cover and bake for one hour. Remove from oven and cool for five minutes.

Bison Wild Burgers

Who needs fast food when these tasty burgers are being served up? Slather with Paleo condiments (see chapter 11) and wrap in lettuce leaves, and you will be in burger heaven.
SERVES 4

> 2 tablespoons extra virgin olive oil
> 1 medium yellow onion, diced
> 1 fennel bulb, fronds removed, cored and diced
> 1 medium tomato, seeded and diced
> 1½ pounds ground bison
> 1 omega 3 egg
> 4 large Bibb or butter lettuce leaves
> 1 large red heirloom tomato, thickly sliced

Preheat oven to broil.

Heat oil in a cast iron skillet over medium flame. Add onion and fennel and sauté for five minutes. Toss in diced tomato and continue to sauté for three minutes. Remove from flame and set aside to cool for ten minutes.

Place mixture in food processor and lightly blend until ingredients appear slightly chopped. Combine bison with egg and mix thoroughly. Add onion mixture to bison and shape into four equal patties.

Place patties on wire rack and broil for twenty minutes, turning at the halfway point. Place patties in large Bibb or butter lettuce leaves, and top with tomato slices and the Paleo condiments of your choice (see chapter 11 for recipes).

Bison Steak with Caramelized Onions

The proven benefits of eating grass-fed bison have us convinced that this meat dish should become a regular part of your Paleo meals. Whether you serve this for breakfast, lunch, or dinner, your body will thank you for this powerful protein indulgence. SERVES 4

2 tablespoons extra virgin olive oil
1 large Vidalia onion, sliced into thick rings
1 tablespoon freshly squeezed orange juice
4 bison filet mignon steaks, 4–6 ounces each
2 tablespoons chopped fresh parsley

In a cast iron skillet, heat 1 tablespoon of the oil over medium flame. Add onion rings and cook for five minutes, turning at the halfway point for even browning. Pour in orange juice and continue cooking for one minute. Remove onions from pan, place in bowl, and cover with foil to keep warm.

Add the remaining tablespoon of oil to skillet and add steaks, cooking for five minutes on each side. Remove from pan and tent with foil for five minutes. Top steaks with onions and parsley.

Shiitake Meat Loaf

This meat loaf is sure to please everyone at your Paleo dinner table. You will love the hearty flavor of this dish, made with only the healthiest ingredients. SERVES 4

1 tablespoon extra virgin olive oil
¼ cup sliced shiitake mushrooms
2 plum tomatoes, chopped
1½ pounds ground grass-fed beef or bison
1 omega 3 egg
1 tablespoon freshly ground flaxseed
½ teaspoon onion powder
½ teaspoon garlic powder
¼ cup red wine

Preheat oven to 350 degrees.

Heat oil in a cast iron skillet over medium flame. Add mushrooms and cook for five minutes. Toss in tomatoes and cook for an additional five minutes. Remove from heat and cool for five minutes. Purée in food processor.

Combine meat, egg, flaxseed, onion powder, garlic powder, and tomato mixture in a medium bowl and mix thoroughly. Place mixture in loaf pan. Drizzle with wine.

Bake meat loaf for one hour and fifteen minutes. Remove from oven and cool for five minutes.

William Cody's Barbecued Bison Ribs

We recommend that you avoid fatty beef ribs from corn-raised, feedlot-produced cattle. Here is a pleasant alternative. Just like lamb chops from grass-fed animals, these delectable treats are high-protein foods enriched with healthy fats including DHA, EPA, monounsaturated fats, and stearic acid. Indulge and enjoy! SERVES 4

12 free-range bison ribs
1 teaspoon dried rosemary
1 teaspoon dried thyme
1 teaspoon dried basil
2 dried bay leaves
2 garlic cloves, minced
1 cup Raspberry Barbecue Sauce (page 200)

Separate ribs with a sharp carving knife.

In a large stockpot, heat 4 quarts of water over high flame. Combine rosemary, thyme, basil, bay leaves, and garlic in a small bowl and add to water. Place ribs in pot and bring to a boil. Reduce flame to low and simmer for ten minutes.

Remove ribs and place in a large bowl. Ignite grill to medium flame. Brush ribs thoroughly with barbecue sauce and place on grill. Cook for fifteen minutes, turning and basting throughout the cooking process to avoid scorching.

Elk Tenderloin in Cherry Reduction

As avid hunters know, elk meat is one of the sweetest of all wild game. For those of us who do our hunting in the aisles of the grocery store, elk meat is beginning to be available for purchase. Give it a try. We're sure you will soon make this a regular meal at your Paleo table. SERVES 4

2 tablespoons extra virgin olive oil
4 elk tenderloin medallions, 4–6 ounces each
1 small onion, chopped
1 cup diced cremini mushrooms
1 shallot, thinly sliced
1 cup chopped Rainier or Bing cherries
½ cup red wine

In a cast iron skillet, heat 1 tablespoon of the olive oil over medium flame. Add medallions and cook for three minutes on each side. Remove from pan and tent with foil.

Add the remaining tablespoon of oil to pan. Place onion, mushrooms, and shallot in pan and sauté for five minutes. Add the cherries and continue cooking for five minutes.

Turn flame to high and add wine. Scrape browned bits from bottom of pan and cook for two minutes to reduce liquid. Top steaks with cherry mixture.

Ostrich Almondine

You will instantly love this unusual protein source. Many natural food stores are making this delicacy available for purchase. Paleo fans enjoy serving this dish to celebrate a special occasion. SERVES 4

2 tablespoons extra virgin olive oil
2 medium shallots, minced
4 large garlic cloves, minced
4 ostrich medallions, 4–6 ounces each
2 tablespoons brandy (optional)
2 tablespoons slivered roasted almonds

Heat oil in a cast iron skillet over medium flame. Add shallots and garlic and sauté for three minutes.

Place ostrich medallions in skillet and cook for eight minutes, turning at halfway point. Turn flame to high and pour in optional brandy. Sauté for one minute. Remove from heat and sprinkle with almonds.

Paleo Warrior's Jerky

Making jerky requires a food dehydrator and a jerky gun, which can be purchased at stores where cooking products are sold. Our teenage sons make this Paleo-perfect snack regularly and prefer it to the salt-laden store-bought version. MAKES 1 POUND

1 pound grass-fed ground beef or bison*
1 tablespoon freshly ground black pepper
2 teaspoons cayenne pepper
1 tablespoon ground cumin
1 tablespoon garlic powder
1 tablespoon onion powder
1 tablespoon paprika

In a large bowl, thoroughly mix all ingredients. Cover and store in the refrigerator for one to two days.

Stuff jerky gun with mixture and squirt onto dehydrator trays. Strips should be 2–3 inches long.

Set dehydrator on meat setting and dry for eight to ten hours. Check jerky throughout process to ensure your personal taste for dryness.

*NOTE: Some people prefer to substitute beef or bison roast. Slice it into thin strips, mix thoroughly with spices, and dry in dehydrator.

8

Paleo Fish and Seafood

One of the absolutely essential elements of the Paleo Diet is to increase your consumption of foods containing the long-chain omega 3 fatty acids known as EPA and DHA. Your best sources of these vital nutrients are fatty fish like salmon, mackerel, sardines, and herring. A 100-gram (~ ¼ pound) serving of salmon contains ~ 1,200 milligrams of EPA and DHA. If you're like most Americans, your normal daily diet only provides between 100 and 200 milligrams of these healthy fatty acids.

Try to consume at least 500 to 1,800 milligrams of EPA + DHA a day, either by eating fish or by taking fish oil supplements. If you have cardiovascular disease, you should include at least 1 gram of EPA + DHA in your diet. Patients with high blood triglycerides can lower these by as much as 40 percent by taking 2 to 4 grams of EPA + DHA daily. The table below shows the levels of omega 3 fatty acids in common types of fish and shellfish.

OMEGA-3 CONTENT OF SEAFOOD PER 100-GRAM PORTIONS

ALA = alpha linolenic acid (18:3n3)
EPA = eicosapentaenoic acid (20:5n3)
DHA = docosahexaenoic acid (22:6n3)
Tr = Trace amount

	ALA (Grams)	EPA (Grams)	DHA (Grams)	Total
Fish				
Anchovy, European	0.5	0.9	1.4	2.8
Bass, freshwater	Tr	0.1	0.2	0.3
Bass, striped	Tr	0.2	0.6	0.8
Bluefish	0.4	0.8	1.2	2.4
Carp	0.3	0.2	0.1	0.6
Catfish, brown bullhead	0.1	0.2	0.2	0.5
Catfish, channel	Tr	0.1	0.2	0.3
Cod, Atlantic	Tr	0.1	0.2	0.3
Cod, Pacific	Tr	0.1	0.1	0.2

	ALA (Grams)	EPA (Grams)	DHA (Grams)	Total
Croaker, Atlantic	Tr	0.1	0.1	0.2
Eel, European	0.7	0.1	0.1	0.9
Flounder, unspecified	Tr	0.1	0.1	0.2
Grouper	Tr	Tr	0.3	0.3
Haddock	Tr	0.1	0.1	0.2
Halibut, Greenland	Tr	0.5	0.4	0.9
Halibut, Pacific	0.1	0.1	0.3	0.5
Herring, Atlantic	0.1	0.7	0.9	1.7
Herring, Pacific	0.1	1.0	0.7	1.8
Mackerel, Atlantic	0.1	0.9	1.6	2.6
Mackerel, king	—	1.0	1.2	2.2
Mullet, unspecified	Tr	0.5	0.6	1.1
Ocean perch	Tr	0.1	0.1	0.2
Perch, white	0.1	0.2	0.1	0.4
Perch, yellow	Tr	0.1	0.2	0.3
Pike, northern	Tr	Tr	0.1	0.1
Pollock	—	0.1	0.4	0.5
Pompano, Florida	—	0.2	0.4	0.6
Rockfish, unspecified	Tr	0.2	0.3	0.5
Salmon, Atlantic	0.2	0.3	0.9	1.4
Salmon, chinook	0.1	0.8	0.6	1.5
Salmon, chum	0.1	0.4	0.6	1.1
Salmon, coho	0.2	0.3	0.5	1.0
Salmon, pink	Tr	0.4	0.6	1.0
Salmon, sockeye	0.1	0.5	0.7	1.3
Sea trout, sand	Tr	0.1	0.2	0.3
Shark, unspecified	—	Tr	0.5	0.5
Smelt, rainbow	0.1	0.3	0.4	0.8
Snapper, red	Tr	Tr	0.2	0.2
Sole, European	Tr	Tr	0.1	0.1
Sturgeon, common	0.1	0.2	0.1	0.4
Sunfish, pumpkinseed	Tr	Tr	0.1	0.1
Swordfish	—	0.1	0.1	0.2
Trout, Arctic char	Tr	0.1	0.5	0.6
Trout, brook	0.2	0.2	0.2	0.6

(continued)

(continued)

	ALA (Grams)	EPA (Grams)	DHA (Grams)	Total
Trout, lake	0.4	0.5	1.1	2.0
Trout, rainbow	0.1	0.1	0.4	0.6
Tuna, albacore	0.2	0.3	1.0	1.5
Tuna, bluefin	—	0.4	1.2	1.6
Tuna, skipjack	0.1	0.3	0.4	0.8
Walleye	Tr	0.1	0.2	0.3
Whitefish, lake	0.2	0.3	1.0	1.5
Crustaceans				
Crab, Alaska king	Tr	0.2	0.1	0.3
Crab, blue	Tr	0.2	0.2	0.4
Crab, Dungeness	—	0.2	0.1	0.3
Crayfish, unspecified	Tr	0.1	Tr	0.1
Lobster, northern	0.1	0.1	0.2	0.4
Lobster, spiny Caribbean	Tr	0.2	0.1	0.3
Shrimp, unspecified	Tr	0.2	0.1	0.3
Mollusks				
Abalone, South African	Tr	Tr	Tr	0.0
Clam, littleneck	Tr	Tr	Tr	0.0
Clam, softshell	Tr	0.2	0.2	0.4
Mussel, blue	Tr	0.2	0.3	0.5
Octopus, common	—	0.1	0.1	0.2
Oyster, eastern	Tr	0.2	0.2	0.4
Oyster, Pacific	Tr	0.4	0.2	0.6
Scallop, unspecified	Tr	0.1	0.1	0.2
Squid, unspecified	Tr	0.1	0.2	0.3

Source: *J. Exler and J. L. Wehrauch, "Provisional Table on the Content of Omega-3 Fatty Acids and Other Fat Components in Selected Foods," U.S. Department of Agriculture Human Nutrition Information Service, HNS/PT-103, 1988.*

In the past decade, perhaps the single most important dietary recommendation to improve your health and prevent chronic disease is to increase your dietary intake of EPA + DHA. Thousands of scientific papers on a variety of diseases unmistakably show the health benefits of these fatty acids. In randomized clinical trials in patients with preexisting heart disease, omega 3 fatty acid supplements significantly reduced cardiovascular events (deaths, nonfatal heart attacks, and nonfatal strokes). Omega 3 fatty acids diminish the risk for heart disease through a number of means, including a reduction in heartbeat irregularities called arrhythmias, a decrease in blood clots, and a reduction in inflammation, a condition that is now known to be an important cause of atherosclerosis, or artery clogging.

Besides lowering the risk for heart disease, regular consumption of fish or supplemental omega 3 fatty acids may be helpful in preventing, treating, or improving a wide variety of diseases and disorders, including virtually all inflammatory diseases (any disease ending with "-itis"): rheumatoid arthritis, inflammatory bowel disorders (Crohn's disease, ulcerative colitis), and periodontal disease (gingivitis).

In addition, mental disorders (including autism, depression, postpartum depression, bipolar disorder, borderline personality disorder, and impaired cognitive development in infants and children) respond positively to these healthy fatty acids.

Finally, acne, asthma, exercise-induced asthma, many types of cancers, macular degeneration, preterm birth, psoriasis, insulin resistance, type 1 diabetes, type 2 diabetes, cancer cachexia, intermittent claudication, skin damage from sunlight, IgA nephropathy, lupus erythematosus, multiple sclerosis, and migraine headaches also improve with omega 3 fatty acids.

Wow! What a list! Have I missed anything?

More important, fish and seafood just taste good. Think about the endless possibilities of how these high-protein, low-fat, omega 3–enriched foods can be incorporated into the Paleo Diet. One of my favorites is cold steamed crab legs for breakfast along with some seasonal fruit. What better way to start your day than with low-fat, high-protein seafood and a delicious serving of fruit? You will be energized all morning long, and this combo of modern-day Paleo foods will reduce your appetite and help the pounds melt away effortlessly.

Cedar-Plank Salmon

This omega 3–, vitamin-, and mineral-packed recipe offers a simple way to impart the taste of fireside cooking indoors.
SERVES 4

1 pound wild Alaskan king salmon fillet
2 tablespoons extra virgin olive oil
1 tablespoon freshly squeezed lemon juice
1 tablespoon dried dill weed
1 tablespoon paprika
4 large fresh basil leaves
1 cedar plank, soaked in water for 1 hour
Freshly ground black pepper, to taste

Preheat oven to 425 degrees.

Cover the flesh side (not the skin) of the salmon with 1 tablespoon of the olive oil and the lemon juice. Sprinkle with dill and paprika. Press the basil leaves lightly onto the flesh.

Place fillet, flesh side down, on plank. Rub the remaining tablespoon of olive oil on the skin. Bake for fifteen to twenty minutes, depending on the thickness of the fish. Check that the salmon is done by lightly flaking with a fork.

Remove from oven, tent with foil, and set aside for five minutes. Turn skin side down and sprinkle with freshly ground black pepper.

Chilean Sea Bass en Papillote

The secret to the incredible flavors in this dish is the use of parchment paper to wrap and seal the fish. This is a great recipe to prepare for special guests. You'll have them thinking you've spent hours cooking when in reality you were only in the kitchen for thirty minutes. SERVES 4

4 large carrots
2 leeks, roots and top green portions removed
4 pieces parchment paper
4 6-ounce Chilean sea bass steaks
4 tablespoons extra virgin olive oil
2 tablespoons dry white wine
2 tablespoons freshly squeezed lemon juice
1 teaspoon garlic powder
1 tablespoon dried dill weed
1 teaspoon freshly ground black pepper

Preheat oven to 425 degrees.

Peel carrots and cut into matchsticks. Cut leeks into matchstick pieces to match carrots. Cut each piece of parchment paper into a 12-inch square. Place equal amounts of carrots and leeks on each of the four squares.

Place one sea bass steak on top of each mound of veggies. Combine 1 tablespoon oil, ½ tablespoon (1½ teaspoons) wine, and ½ tablespoon lemon juice and drizzle the mixture over each piece of fish. Sprinkle with garlic powder, dill, and black pepper. Gather the sides of each parchment square together and tie with a piece of kitchen twine.

Bake for fifteen to twenty minutes, depending on the thickness of the fish. Open parchment and transfer fish and veggies to plates.

Barramundi Vegetable Soup

This unique recipe combines fish with a flavorful soup to warm you up on a chilly day. Enjoy with your favorite Paleo salad (see chapter 9) for a vitamin- and protein-packed meal. SERVES 4

2 tablespoons extra virgin olive oil

4 4-ounce barramundi (sea bass) fillets

½ cup chopped oyster mushrooms

1 medium shallot, chopped

2 large carrots, chopped into 1-inch pieces

2 large zucchini, chopped into 1-inch pieces

2 plum tomatoes, seeded and chopped

2 cups Chicken Broth (page 193)

2 tablespoons chopped fresh parsley

4 lemon wedges

Cayenne pepper, to taste

Preheat oven to 160 degrees.

Heat 1 tablespoon of the oil in a cast iron skillet over medium flame. Add fish and cook for three minutes, skin side up. Turn and continue cooking for one minute. Remove from pan and place in baking dish. Cover and place in oven to keep warm.

Pour the remaining tablespoon of oil into pan. Add mushrooms and cook for five minutes. Stir in shallot and continue cooking for one minute. Place carrots, zucchini, and tomatoes into pan and cook for two minutes, stirring once to brown evenly. Pour in broth. Turn heat to high and bring to boil. Cover, reduce heat, and simmer for twenty minutes.

Pour soup into bowls and top with fish. Garnish with parsley, lemon wedges, and cayenne pepper.

Peach and Ginger Scallops

These flavorful morsels are a gift from the sea. The mild flavor of the scallops infused with the sweet and spicy flavors of the other distinctive ingredients produces a mouthwatering dish.
SERVES 4

2 tablespoons extra virgin olive oil
1 large shallot, minced
1 tablespoon freshly grated ginger root
2 large peaches, peeled, cored, and coarsely chopped
2 pounds sea scallops
Juice from ½ lime

Heat 1 tablespoon of the oil in a cast iron skillet over medium flame. Add shallot and cook for two minutes. Combine with ginger and stir for half a minute.

Place peaches in skillet and continue cooking for three minutes, stirring at the halfway point. Remove peach mixture and place in a small bowl. Cover to keep warm.

Add the remaining tablespoon of oil to skillet. Place scallops in a single layer and cook for four to six minutes, turning once. Return peach mixture to pan, covering shallots evenly. Remove from heat and drizzle with lime juice.

Grilled Snapper

The flavors in this dish do indeed snap your senses to attention. It's perfect for any meal, but for Paleo Dieters who love fish for breakfast, this meal can be made quickly and easily to help start your day off right. SERVES 4

½ teaspoon oregano
½ teaspoon marjoram
½ teaspoon paprika
½ teaspoon white pepper
½ teaspoon turmeric
2 tablespoons extra virgin olive oil
4 red snapper fillets, 4–6 ounces each

Set grill to medium flame or preheat oven to broil.

Combine oregano, marjoram, paprika, white pepper, and turmeric in a small bowl. Brush oil onto fillets and coat them evenly with spice mixture.

Grill or broil for eight minutes, turning at the halfway point.

Richard's Braised River Trout

A fisherman's favorite, trout can now be bought in most super-markets. Most available trout, however, is farm-raised and fat-tened on cereal grains, which significantly reduces the level of omega 3. Whenever possible, get wild fish to ensure the most nutritious meal possible. SERVES 4

2 tablespoons extra virgin olive oil
2 large leeks
2 large carrots, peeled and diced

1 cup Chicken Broth (page 193)
4 river trout fillets, 4–6 ounces each
Freshly ground black pepper, to taste

Heat oil in a cast iron skillet over medium flame. Remove roots and green top portions from leeks and dice. Place in skillet and sauté with carrots for four minutes, turning once.

Pour in chicken broth and bring to a boil. Reduce heat and simmer for ten minutes.

Add trout to pan, cover, and cook for five minutes. Sprinkle with pepper to taste.

Pan-Seared Branzino

This sea bass, found in northern Italian waters, offers a subtle flavor while providing you with a great source of omega 3s.

SERVES 4

2 tablespoons extra virgin olive oil
1 small yellow onion, diced
2 large plum tomatoes, seeded and diced
4 branzino fillets, 4–6 ounces each
¼ cup minced fresh basil
Freshly ground white pepper, to taste

Heat oil in a cast iron skillet over medium flame. Add onion and sauté for five minutes. Place tomatoes in skillet and continue cooking for five minutes.

Move tomato and onion to side of pan and add fillets, skin side down. Cook for five minutes and turn once. Turn skin side down again and top with tomatoes and onion.

Sprinkle with basil and dust lightly with freshly ground pepper.

Soulful Sole

The unique pairing of pork with the mellow flavor of fish makes a flavorful dish reminiscent of Southern cooking and surf and turf. You'll enjoy the down-home taste of this easy-to-prepare meal. SERVES 4

2 tablespoons extra virgin olive oil

1 ounce leftover pork tenderloin, diced

2 scallions, diced

1 teaspoon nutmeg

1 teaspoon dried thyme

1 teaspoon garlic powder

½ teaspoon ground cloves

Cayenne pepper, to taste

4 6-ounce sole fillets

Heat oil in a cast iron skillet over medium flame. Add pork and scallions. Sauté for three minutes.

Combine nutmeg, thyme, garlic powder, cloves, and cayenne pepper in a small dish. Sprinkle fillets with spice mixture, evenly coating each side. Place in pan with pork and cook for four minutes, turning at the halfway point.

Poached Halibut

Lorrie discovered this succulent fish while working in Alaska. Its tender white meat has become a family favorite. SERVES 4

2 lemons, 1 sliced into rounds, 1 cut into wedges

4 halibut fillets, 4–6 ounces each

2 tablespoons cold-pressed flaxseed oil

1 tablespoon fresh dill

1 tablespoon freshly ground black pepper

1 tablespoon garlic powder

4 lemon wedges

Insert steamer basket in a 4-quart pot and fill with 1 inch of water. Place lemon slices in basket and bring to a boil. Layer with halibut, reduce heat to low, and simmer for ten minutes. Remove from pan.

Drizzle halibut with flaxseed oil, followed by dill, pepper, and garlic powder. Garnish with lemon wedges.

Paleo Crab Cakes

We believe that we've created the perfect recipe for Paleo Dieters who enjoy this treat from the sea. Try this yummy omega 3 dish prepared without grains and dairy. SERVES 4

1½ pounds fresh crabmeat

1 small shallot, minced

2 scallions, minced

1 tablespoon minced fresh cilantro, plus 4 sprigs

2 tablespoons freshly ground flaxseed meal

2 omega 3 eggs

2 tablespoons extra virgin olive oil

4 lemon wedges

Freshly ground black pepper, to taste

Combine crabmeat in a food processor with shallot, scallions, and minced cilantro and process until smooth.

Place crab mixture in a bowl and combine thoroughly with flaxseed meal and eggs. Shape into four patties.

Heat oil in a cast iron skillet over medium flame. Cook patties for eight minutes, turning them once. Garnish with lemon wedges and cilantro sprigs. Sprinkle with pepper.

Broiled Lobster Tail

Many grocery stores and fish markets keep live lobsters in large tanks, so you can purchase them fresh. This Paleo-favorite seafood treat is sure to impress your family and friends. SERVES 4

4 small fresh lobster tails
1 lemon, ½ juiced, ½ cut into 4 wedges
2 tablespoons minced fresh parsley
Freshly ground black pepper, to taste

Preheat oven to broil. With a sharp knife, slice vertically down the backs of the lobster tails and pull them slightly apart. Sprinkle with lemon juice, parsley, and pepper.

Broil for eight to ten minutes until the meat is opaque. Garnish with lemon wedges.

Roasted Swordfish with Mushroom Medley

Wild mushrooms and fresh seasonings fill this dish with subtle flavors and a fresh-from-the-ocean taste. Enjoy with a light salad and fruit to complete the experience. SERVES 4

4 swordfish steaks, 4–6 ounces each
2 tablespoons extra virgin olive oil
1 cup mixed wild mushrooms (try porcini, cremini, and shiitake)
1 medium shallot, minced
2 garlic cloves, minced
1 tablespoon fresh parsley, minced
¼ cup dry white wine

Preheat oven to 425 degrees.

Heat 1 tablespoon of the oil in a cast iron skillet over medium flame. Add mushrooms and cook for five minutes. Toss in shallot and cook for one additional minute. Add garlic and stir for half a minute.

Stir in parsley and wine and bring to a boil. Scrape browned bits from surface of skillet and mix with liquid. Remove from heat.

Move mushroom mixture to sides of skillet, making room for fish in the center. Place fish in skillet and drizzle with the remaining tablespoon of olive oil. Smother with mushroom mix and cover. Bake for fifteen minutes.

Wild Salmon Basil Burgers

These seafood burgers are sure to be a big hit at your next barbecue. Cook them on the grill or broil them in the oven for a mouthwatering delight. SERVES 4

> 1½ pounds boneless wild king salmon fillet
> ¼ cup minced fresh basil
> 1 garlic clove, minced
> 1 omega 3 egg
> 1 teaspoon onion powder

Heat grill to medium or oven to broil.

Place salmon in a food processor with basil and garlic and blend until smooth. Place mixture in a medium bowl. Combine with egg and onion powder and shape into patties. Cook for fifteen minutes, turning once.

Dress with your favorite Paleo condiment (see chapter 11) and wrap with lettuce leaves.

Paleo Shrimp Delight

Our Paleo friends rave about this recipe. The garlic and lime infusion makes a delicious dish with little effort. You can almost hear the waves. SERVES 4

2 pounds jumbo shrimp, unpeeled
1 tablespoon freshly squeezed lime juice
2 tablespoons extra virgin olive oil
1 garlic clove, minced
4 small plum tomatoes, seeded and sliced into very thin wedges
½ cup shredded fresh basil
1 lime, quartered

Using kitchen shears, cut a thin slice down the backs of each shrimp, leaving peel on. Snip shrimp legs with shears. Gently toss shrimp with lime juice and set aside.

Heat oil in a cast iron skillet over medium flame. Add garlic and cook for thirty seconds. Layer with shrimp and cook for two minutes; turn once. Add tomatoes and cook for two minutes; stir at the halfway point. Garnish with basil and lime quarters.

Diablo Crab Legs

The devil is in the details for this spicy recipe. The dipping sauce makes a perfect complement for the nutrition-packed crab. Enjoy with a fresh Paleo salad and fruit to complete your meal. SERVES 4

2 Alaskan king crab legs
2 tablespoons extra virgin olive oil
1 medium yellow onion, diced

1 jalapeño pepper, diced

2 plum tomatoes, seeded and chopped

6 garlic cloves, crushed

1 teaspoon cayenne pepper

Fill a large stockpot with water and bring to a boil. Place crab legs in water and cook for six minutes.

Heat oil in a cast iron skillet over medium flame. Add onion and cook for five minutes. Stir in pepper and tomatoes and continue cooking for two minutes. Sprinkle with garlic and cayenne pepper and remove from heat.

Puree tomato-garlic mixture in a food processor to make dipping sauce for crab legs.

Paleo Spicy Tuna Rolls

Sushi has quickly become a favorite food for seafood lovers. The unique flavors of this simple recipe are designed with Paleo Dieters in mind. You'll never miss the rice, the salt, and the unhealthy additives. SERVES 4

1½ pounds sushi-grade ahi tuna, cubed

2 tablespoons cold-pressed flaxseed oil

2 teaspoons cayenne pepper

1 teaspoon freshly grated ginger root

4 nori (seaweed) sheets

Place tuna, oil, pepper, and ginger in a food processor. Blend until thoroughly combined.

Lay sheets of nori on a work surface. Spread a quarter of the tuna mixture in a triangle shape on one corner of each sheet, leaving 1 inch uncovered. Roll into cone shape.

Salmon Fillet with Nectarine Infusion

The sweet taste of nectarine makes this dish a regular favorite in the Paleo home. Your omega 3 requirements will easily be met by eating this delicious dish. SERVES 4

2 tablespoons minced fresh cilantro

2 tablespoons minced red onion

2 tablespoons freshly squeezed lime juice

4 wild salmon fillets

2 tablespoons extra virgin olive oil

1 large nectarine, cut into very thin wedges

Preheat oven to 425 degrees.

Combine cilantro, onion, and lime juice in a small bowl. Brush skin side of salmon with 1 tablespoon of the oil.

Place fish, skin side down, on a wire rack. Press nectarine wedges evenly onto salmon flesh and cover thoroughly with lime mixture. Drizzle with the remaining tablespoon of olive oil and bake for fifteen minutes.

Shrimp and Pineapple Skewers

This shrimp kebab will delight your family and friends. The sweet and succulent flavors will surely be a hit at your next backyard barbecue. SERVES 4

2 pounds medium shrimp, shells removed

4 wooden skewers, soaked in water for one hour

8 ounces fresh pineapple, cubed

1 tablespoon extra virgin olive oil

1 tablespoon freshly squeezed lime juice
1 tablespoon minced fresh cilantro
1 teaspoon chili powder
1 tablespoon cold-pressed flaxseed oil

Ignite grill to medium or preheat oven to broil. Thread shrimp and pineapple evenly onto skewers.

Combine olive oil with lime juice, cilantro, and chili powder. Drizzle over skewers. Cook for eight minutes, turning once. Remove from heat and drizzle with flaxseed oil.

Sweet and Savory Swordfish

If something different is what you're looking for, this scrumptious treat from the sea is the perfect choice. Tender and juicy with just the right spices, this omega 3 meal will make your palate jump for joy. SERVES 4

2 tablespoons extra virgin olive oil
2 tablespoons minced ginger root, unpeeled
4 garlic cloves, minced
Juice from 1 lime
2 teaspoons chili powder
4 6-ounce wild swordfish steaks

Preheat oven to broil.

Combine oil, ginger, garlic, lime juice, and chili powder in a small bowl and mix well.

Evenly coat the surface of a 9½ × 11-inch baking dish with half of the ginger mixture. Add fish and cover with the remaining mixture. Place in oven and broil for fifteen minutes, turning at the halfway point.

Paleo Tilapia Tacos

The use of lettuce leaves in lieu of traditional taco shells allows you to enjoy this seaside treat in a healthy way. Try it with your favorite Paleo salsa (see chapter 11) for an extra spicy kick.
SERVES 4

> 4 6-ounce tilapia fillets
> Cayenne pepper, to taste
> 2 tablespoons extra virgin olive oil
> 1 red bell pepper, thinly sliced
> 2 scallions, diced
> 2 garlic cloves, minced
> 2 tablespoons chopped fresh cilantro
> 4 Bibb or butter lettuce leaves
> 1 small avocado, thinly sliced

Season tilapia with cayenne pepper, and set aside.

Heat oil in a cast iron skillet over medium flame. Add pepper and scallions. Sauté for three minutes. Toss in garlic and continue cooking for one minute.

Move veggies to sides of pan, making room for fish in the center. Add fish to pan and cook for four minutes, turning at the halfway point.

Remove fish from pan and cut into bite-sized pieces. Cover with veggies and sprinkle with cilantro. Carefully scoop into lettuce leaves and top with avocado slices.

9

Paleo Salads

Salads of all kinds are wonderful additions to modern-day Paleo Diets, and most foods and ingredients that we throw into these mouthwatering combos are pure Paleo, meaning they are raw, fresh, tasty, and nutritious. "Honeymoon salad" (lettuce alone) with Thousand Island dressing is a fallback to an era when children were fed cornflakes for breakfast and bologna sandwiches with mayonnaise on white bread for lunch. Be creative as you fashion Paleo salads from scratch, and realize that the rules are dictated only by what is good for you and what tastes good.

We often get into ruts and think that salads can be made only of greens and fresh veggies. Nothing could be further from the truth. The creative aspect of the Paleo Diet cuisine is the incredible diversity of delicious ingredients that can be incorporated into almost any salad. Feel free to add meat, fish, shellfish, and fruit to your salads, but keep in mind that the more ingredients you consider, the more complicated things can get. Using what is in season makes it easier to narrow the possibilities. Don't be tempted to unload your veggie drawer and throw its limp celery and dilapidated carrots into the mix. Always try to get the freshest ingredients possible. One trick is to wash your veggies as soon as you get them home, then store them in closed plastic bags in the fridge.

The salad, which has been around at least since Roman times, continues to change its character, forever finding new ways to be reinvented with adaptable mixes of loosely related elements, not necessarily vegetables, unified by a dressing. As you become creative with Paleo salads, try to put together ingredients that are not only pleasing to the palate but also attractive to the eye.

Texture can make or break a salad. Try to incorporate tasty pearls that add flavor, color, and texture into the mix. For example, blanched asparagus spears sliced into tiny rounds and added to a bowl of shredded romaine lettuce, with chopped tarragon and a little arugula for spiciness, make a great starting point for an appetizing and eye-catching salad.

Salads may be served at any point during a meal, and they can perform numerous functions, including:

- Appetizer salads, to stimulate the palate as the first course of the meal
- Side salads, to accompany the entrée
- Entrée salads, served as the main dish and usually containing meat or seafood
- Palate-cleansing salads, after the main course (this is the way salads are usually served in Europe)
- Dessert salads, usually made with fresh and dried fruit

However you eat a healthy salad, it's all good. Paleo salads can serve as small tasty items before a meal, or they can serve as filling meals on their own, especially with added nuts, seeds, and omega 3–enriched eggs. Do yourself a favor and try to eat a Paleo salad every day!

Arugula-Avocado Salad

Serve this salad alongside any Paleo dish. Your friends and family will enjoy the sweet, savory, and nutty combination of flavors. SERVES 4

4 cups fresh arugula
1 tablespoon extra virgin olive oil
1 tablespoon cold-pressed flaxseed oil
½ teaspoon dried dill
½ teaspoon freshly squeezed lemon juice
1 large avocado, cut into 8 slices
1 pint fresh raspberries
2 tablespoons chopped raw walnuts

Combine arugula, oils, dill, and lemon juice in a medium bowl and toss to mix thoroughly. Place equal portions on four plates.

Top with avocado slices and raspberries. Scatter with walnuts.

French Country Salad

French countryside cooking is usually hearty and flavorful. You'll often find a main dish paired with a simple fresh salad. Using local greens allows you to experience lettuce leaves and herbs that are delicate and mild. SERVES 4

2 small heads Bibb or butter lettuce, torn
1 tablespoon minced fresh parsley
1 tablespoon minced fresh oregano
1 teaspoon crushed mustard seed
1 teaspoon freshly squeezed lemon juice

1 tablespoon extra virgin olive oil

1 tablespoon walnut oil

Freshly ground pepper, to taste

Place lettuce in large salad bowl. Combine parsley, oregano, mustard, lemon juice, and oils in a small jar. Shake well.

Toss with lettuce and sprinkle with freshly ground pepper.

Paleo Caprese Salad

This light, easy-to-make summer salad is a variation of the traditional mozzarella version. Using fresh, in-season, local heirloom tomatoes and basil makes up for any flavors one might miss. Choose your tomatoes based on their smell. A tomato that imparts a lovely garden scent is sure to taste the best. SERVES 4

1 large red heirloom tomato, cut into ¼-inch slices

1 large yellow or green heirloom tomato, cut into
  ¼-inch slices

2 tablespoons extra virgin olive oil

4 large fresh basil leaves, coarsely chopped

1 small red onion, thinly sliced

Freshly ground black pepper, to taste

Arrange tomato slices on a platter, drizzle with olive oil, and scatter with basil. Cover with onion slices. Add freshly ground black pepper.

NOTE: This is one recipe in which making extra is not advised. Refrigerating cut tomatoes tends to leave them mushy and unappealing.

Paleo Tuna Niçoise

You'll love the tasty combination of flavors, and this salad will become a frequent flyer on your lunch or dinner table.
SERVES 4

4 4-ounce tuna steaks
2 tablespoons chopped fresh rosemary
1 garlic clove, crushed
2 tablespoons red wine
2 tablespoons extra virgin olive oil
4 cups mâche (lamb's lettuce)
2 hard-boiled eggs, quartered
8 cherry tomatoes
Freshly ground pepper, to taste

Place tuna in an oiled glass baking dish. Combine rosemary, garlic, red wine, and 1 tablespoon of the olive oil in a jar and shake well. Pour over tuna. Cover and refrigerate for thirty minutes.

Preheat oven to broil. Remove tuna from refrigerator. Broil for twenty minutes, turning at the halfway point. Remove from oven and set aside to cool for ten minutes.

Combine lettuce and the remaining tablespoon of olive oil in a large bowl and toss well. Arrange lettuce with eggs and cherry tomatoes. Layer with tuna steaks and season with freshly ground black pepper.

Salmon Caesar Salad

Everyone loves a fresh Caesar salad. The omega 3s in this recipe combined with the freshest of ingredients make an ideal dish that will quickly become a regular part of your Paleo meals. SERVES 4

4 6-ounce salmon fillets, skin on
2 tablespoons extra virgin olive oil
2 heads romaine lettuce, chopped
¼ small red onion, diced
2 tablespoons cold-pressed flaxseed oil
1 garlic clove, crushed
1 teaspoon crushed mustard seed
1 tablespoon freshly squeezed lemon juice
Freshly ground black pepper, to taste

Preheat oven to broil. Brush flesh side of salmon fillet with 1 tablespoon of the olive oil. Place in baking pan flesh side down. Brush skin with the remaining tablespoon of olive oil. Broil for fifteen minutes. Remove from oven and set aside.

In a large bowl, mix together lettuce and onion. Combine flaxseed oil, garlic, mustard seed, and lemon juice in a small jar and shake well. Toss with lettuce and onion. Serve topped with salmon fillet and season with freshly ground pepper.

Nutty Beet Salad

Making beets a regular ingredient in your Paleo meals will help to keep your vitamin and mineral levels at their peak. This tasty and versatile veggie is power-packed with iron, potassium, and magnesium. SERVES 4

4 small Roasty Toasty Beets (page 178)
1 large navel orange, peeled, with each segment
  cut in half
2 tablespoons chopped roasted filberts (hazelnuts)
¼ teaspoon ground allspice
1 tablespoon freshly squeezed orange juice
2 tablespoons extra virgin olive oil
1 large avocado, cut into 8 slices

In a medium bowl, combine beets, orange, and filberts. In a small bowl, mix allspice, orange juice, and olive oil.

Top salad with avocado slices and drizzle with dressing.

Citrus-Crab Salad

Shellfish makes a scrumptious addition to any Paleo salad. The fresh and flavorful ingredients in this recipe will keep your heart healthy and your brain sharp. SERVES 4

4 6-ounce crab legs
1 tablespoon extra virgin olive oil
1 tablespoon cold-pressed flaxseed oil
2 scallions, chopped
1 tablespoon chopped red onion

1 small apple, peeled, cored, and diced
1 teaspoon freshly squeezed lemon juice
1 tablespoon chopped fresh chives

Fill a large pot with water and bring to a boil. Place crab legs in pot and boil for five to seven minutes. Remove from water and cool for five minutes.

Break shell and remove crabmeat. Chop into small pieces and place in medium salad bowl. Toss with oils, scallions, onion, and apple. Drizzle with lemon juice and sprinkle with chives.

Cactus Salad

A vitamin- and mineral-packed treat awaits you in this delicious salad. Commonly used in the diets of people living south of the border, the cactus is quickly being recognized for its unique flavor and health benefits. SERVES 4

1 16-ounce jar sliced cactus, thoroughly rinsed to remove excess sodium
1 large tomato, chopped
½ small red onion, diced
¼ cup chopped fresh cilantro
1 tablespoon extra virgin olive oil
1 tablespoon cold-pressed flaxseed oil
1 tablespoon freshly squeezed lime juice

Place cactus strips, tomato, and red onion in a large bowl. Combine cilantro, oils, and lime juice in a small jar and shake well. Pour over cactus and toss to thoroughly coat all ingredients. Refrigerate for thirty minutes.

Greek Salata à la Paleo

Juicy tomato, crunchy cucumber, zesty lemon, and a sprinkle of oregano make for a Paleo-friendly Greek salad. You'll find this salad to be a refreshing way to start your meal. SERVES 4

2 large red beefsteak tomatoes, diced
1 large cucumber, peeled and coarsely chopped
1 large green bell pepper, chopped
2 tablespoons minced fresh oregano
1 tablespoon freshly squeezed lemon juice
3 tablespoons extra virgin olive oil
Freshly ground black pepper, to taste

Combine tomatoes, cucumber, bell pepper, and oregano in a large bowl. Drizzle with lemon juice and oil. Toss to combine. Sprinkle with freshly ground black pepper.

Grilled Chicken Salad

Paleo Dieters know that adding some meat to any green salad transforms it into a vitamin- and protein-packed feast. This salad can be considered a meal in itself. SERVES 4

4 4-ounce chicken cutlets
2 tablespoons extra virgin olive oil
1 teaspoon dried thyme
1 teaspoon dried basil
4 cups mesclun lettuce
½ cup diced cherry tomatoes
2 tablespoons cold-pressed flaxseed oil

1 tablespoon freshly squeezed lemon juice
½ small red onion, very thinly sliced
2 tablespoons pumpkin seeds, toasted
Freshly ground black pepper, to taste

Preheat oven to broil. Brush cutlets with olive oil and sprinkle with thyme and basil.

Place cutlets on wire rack and cook for twenty minutes, turning at the halfway point. Remove from oven and cool for five minutes. Cut chicken into strips and set aside.

Combine lettuce and tomatoes in a large bowl. Pour flaxseed oil and lemon juice into a small jar and shake well. Toss with lettuce and tomatoes. Arrange with onion, pumpkin seeds, and chicken strips. Season with pepper.

Mikey's Mâche Salad

Inspired by a similar salad featuring candied nuts and chèvre, this lighter Paleo version will please your taste buds. The sweetness of the pear plays a delicious counterpart to the kick of the cayenne. SERVES 4

4 cups mâche (lamb's lettuce)
2 tablespoons extra virgin olive oil
1 large pear, cored and thinly sliced
2 ounces pecans, roasted and halved
Cayenne pepper, to taste

Combine lettuce and oil in a large bowl. Place equal portions on four plates. Toss in pear slices and pecans. Season with cayenne pepper.

Mixed Herb Salad

Combining the unique flavors of these fresh herbal ingredients makes a simple yet palate-pleasing side dish. Served with a meat or seafood main course, it is the perfect complement to any Paleo meal. SERVES 4

½ cup fresh basil leaves
½ cup fresh mint leaves
1 cup mâche (lamb's lettuce)
1 cup arugula
2 tablespoons walnut oil
1 tablespoon freshly squeezed lemon juice
4 lemon wedges

Combine basil, mint, lettuce, and arugula in a large bowl. Toss with walnut oil and lemon juice. Garnish with lemon wedges.

Strawberry-Spinach Salad

Spinach salads are a Paleo Diet favorite. The ingredients in this salad will make your taste buds come alive, and the iron and the vitamins will boost your health. SERVES 4

4 cups torn spinach leaves
1 cup hulled and quartered strawberries
2 tablespoons extra virgin olive oil
½ teaspoon finely chopped fresh basil
½ teaspoon freshly ground black pepper
½ teaspoon freshly squeezed lime juice
2 ounces cashews, toasted and chopped

Combine spinach with strawberries in a large salad bowl. In a small jar, combine oil, basil, pepper, and lime juice and shake well. Toss with spinach and berries and sprinkle with cashews.

Glenrock Steak Salad

Pair this salad with your favorite seafood dish, and you will have created an exquisite, Paleo-style surf and turf. The protein alone will have your muscles singing with glee. SERVES 4

2 tablespoons extra virgin olive oil

½ teaspoon cayenne pepper

½ teaspoon ground cumin

½ teaspoon garlic powder

2 tablespoons dry red wine

1½ pounds flank steak, pounded with meat tenderizing tool

4 cups mixed green lettuces

2 tablespoons cold-pressed flaxseed oil

1 tablespoon freshly squeezed lime juice

1 small avocado, cut into 4 slices

½ cup pitted and chopped cherries

Combine olive oil, cayenne pepper, cumin, garlic powder, and red wine in a small jar and shake well. Place steak in large bowl and pour in oil mixture. Cover and refrigerate for a minimum of two hours. Remove from refrigerator thirty minutes before cooking.

Preheat oven to broil. Broil steak for twenty minutes, turning at the halfway point. Remove from oven and set aside.

Place lettuce in a large serving bowl. Combine flaxseed oil and lime juice in a small jar and shake well. Toss with lettuce. Slice steak into strips and arrange on top of salad. Add avocado slices and cherries.

Signature Salad

There is no limit to the amount of imagination and variation you can use to create your personal favorite salads. Here is one combination of sweet and savory fruits and veggies for your consideration. Experiment until you develop your own signature salad. SERVES 4

4 cups wild, organic mixed green lettuces

¼ small red onion, sliced

4 large strawberries, washed and sliced

2 ounces raw pecans

½ medium avocado, sliced

¼ cup raspberries

4 lemon wedges

Olive oil, to taste

Drain washed lettuce in a salad spinner. Place lettuce in a large shallow bowl. Arrange red onions, strawberries, pecans, avocado, and raspberries over lettuce.

Serve with lemon wedges and a decanter of olive oil on the side. Dress salad to taste.

10

Paleo Vegetable Dishes

The abundance and the versatility of vegetables offer infinite tastes, textures, colors, and flavors. Imagine a mouthful of fresh local organic carrots and zucchini with a hint of garlic and a touch of ginger. How about a bite of delicate broccoli and cauliflower florets caramelized with orange zest and a hint of walnut oil? Perhaps a side of thyme-infused squash with tomato and sliced almonds? You can enjoy veggies crisp, fresh, delicious, and cooked with ease.

Preparing vegetables with a light touch ensures that they deliver their nutritional benefits to you in a tasty way. Just because vegetables can be considered nature's preventive medicine doesn't mean they have to taste like medicine. Vegetables are a net alkaline-yielding food, which means that if we eat them, our bodies are far less likely to lose calcium from our bones, which in turn helps us to maintain strong skeletons. On the other hand, diets that are low in vegetables and high in grains, cheeses, and processed salty foods create an acidic condition in the body, which may lead to osteoporosis, high blood pressure, kidney stones, and other diseases of acid-alkali imbalance.

Equally important, vegetables, with their rich supply of vitamins, minerals, phytochemicals, antioxidants, and fiber, play a huge part in helping us fight heart disease and cancer. These Paleo non-starchy carbohydrates also help to normalize blood glucose and insulin levels, which in turn promotes weight loss and decreases your chance of developing type 2 diabetes. In addition, eating these important foods will keep you energized all day long.

The distinction between low carb and low starch is important.

It's one of the significant ways the Paleo Diet differs from other popular diets. Some low-carb diets advise their followers to minimize or eliminate certain, or sometimes all, carbohydrates, including fruits and vegetables. The Paleo Diet offers limitless options for eating nonstarchy veggies and fresh fruit, balanced with lean natural proteins and healthy unrefined fats.

Incorporating vegetables into your diet, combined with eliminating the antinutrients found in grains and legumes, allows your body to absorb all the vitamins and minerals that veggies have to offer. You'll feel satisfied without feeling stuffed. The diversity of vegetables that you may choose from is enormous. Try something new. Have you ever tasted kohlrabi or Belgian endive? How about daikon radishes, bok choy, or bamboo shoots? We encourage you to explore ethnic markets and check out their produce sections. The only vegetables that are taboo on the Paleo Diet are potatoes, all beans, and other legumes, for the reasons previously mentioned. People with autoimmune diseases may want to reread chapter 1, because there are a few additional vegetables that you may want to avoid.

Are you new to the kitchen? Unsure how to use the oven and range? Cooking with vegetables is a great way to test the waters. Because most vegetables can safely be eaten raw, preparing them is easy. You don't have to worry about undercooking them or making a big mistake in the ingredients ratios, as you do with meats or when baking. Vegetable preparation can become something that you and even your kids can learn to do with ease in a very short period. Approach it playfully and plan on having fun with the creation and consumption of every new dish.

Julienned Veggie Stir-Fry

The simple act of cutting veggies julienne style completely revolutionizes the appearance of this quite basic dish. An inexpensive mandolin can be purchased to julienne your veggies, or simply cut them into matchsticks using a sharp knife. An important part of this recipe, and of almost any stir-fry, is to allow the vegetables to brown. Once they are added to the pan, let a minute or so pass without stirring. In the immortal words of Julia Child, "Don't crowd the pan!" SERVES 4

2 tablespoons extra virgin olive oil
1 teaspoon grated fresh ginger
2 scallions, finely chopped
1 tablespoon orange zest
2 garlic cloves, minced
2 large carrots, peeled and julienned
1 red bell pepper, julienned
2 medium yellow squash, julienned
2 medium zucchini, julienned

Heat oil in a cast iron skillet over medium flame and sauté ginger and scallions while stirring for two minutes. Add orange zest and garlic and mix lightly for about one minute. Toss in carrots and peppers. Stir so that all veggies come in contact with the pan at some point and continue browning.

Leave veggies to cook for one additional minute without stirring. Place the squash and zucchini in the pan and mix evenly for one minute. Cover and cook over medium heat for ten minutes; stir once. Veggies are done when tender. Remove from flame and let cool for two minutes.

Spaghetti Squash Italiano

Because there is no room for pasta in the Paleo Diet, spaghetti squash is very handy as a vegetable side dish or as a base for your favorite Paleo sauce or protein. Here's a simple recipe that is tasty enough to be enjoyed alone but uncomplicated enough to be added to a more adventurous meal. SERVES 4

    1 medium spaghetti squash
    1 tablespoon chopped fresh basil
    1 tablespoon dried oregano
    2 tablespoons chopped fresh cilantro
    1 tablespoon extra virgin olive oil
    1 tablespoon flaxseed oil

Preheat oven to 425 degrees. Halve spaghetti squash lengthwise. Using a fork, remove seeds and discard. Fill a large glass or ceramic baking dish with 1 inch of water. Place both squash halves, cut side down, into pan. Bake for forty minutes. Squash is done when skin is easily pierced with a fork.

Remove squash from pan and set aside until cool enough to handle, for five to ten minutes. Using a fork, scrape out the strands of squash, which will now resemble spaghetti, onto a large, flat serving dish. In a small jar, combine basil, oregano, and cilantro with the two oils and shake well. Pour over squash strands and mix well.

Roasted Baby Squash and Carrots

Baby vegetables are fully ripe, miniature vegetables, cultivated to perfection. They often have a sweeter taste than their larger counterparts. Deep green zucchini combined with bright orange carrots makes a lovely presentation. SERVES 4

2 tablespoons extra virgin olive oil

1 or 2 garlic cloves, crushed

8 ounces baby zucchini, cut into ¼-inch rounds

8 ounces baby carrots, sliced in half

1 teaspoon finely chopped fresh dill

1 teaspoon dried thyme

Preheat oven to broil. Combine olive oil with garlic in a glass or ceramic baking dish. Add vegetables and mix in dill and thyme. Broil for ten minutes.

Stir vegetables, then continue broiling for one minute. Vegetables are done when easily pierced with a fork. Cool for five minutes before serving.

Nutty Summer Squash

Sometimes the simplest dishes are the tastiest. A simple prep of steamed squash accented by fresh tomatoes and thyme with a snappy finish of toasted hazelnuts takes just minutes to pre-pare and is a colorful addition to any plate. SERVES 4

2 large zucchini, cut into ½-inch rounds

2 large yellow squash, cut into ½-inch rounds

2 tablespoons flaxseed oil

1 large heirloom tomato, diced

1 tablespoon minced fresh thyme

2 tablespoons minced fresh parsley

2 tablespoons roasted hazelnuts

Fill a 2-quart saucepan with 1 quart of water. Insert steamer and bring water to a boil. Add zucchini and yellow squash and cover. Steam ten minutes and stir once.

Drain squash and place in medium bowl. Add oil and mix well. Toss with tomatoes and sprinkle with thyme, parsley, and hazelnuts.

Sunchoke Sauté

Sunchokes (better known as Jerusalem artichokes) are a great part of the Paleo Diet. They make a delicious substitute for white potatoes without the negative consequences of a high glycemic index and saponin content. This side dish is one easy option. SERVES 4

2 tablespoons extra virgin olive oil

2 garlic cloves, diced

1 tablespoon dried oregano

1 tablespoon minced fresh basil

1 teaspoon dried tarragon

8 ounces sunchokes, peeled and cut into ½-inch slices

1 teaspoon freshly ground black pepper

4 fresh parsley sprigs

Heat oil in a cast iron skillet over medium heat. Add garlic, oregano, basil, and tarragon and stir for one minute. Add sunchokes and continue to stir for eight to ten minutes, or until tender. Remove from heat and sprinkle with pepper. Garnish with sprigs of parsley.

Blasted Veggie Medley

This recipe is based on a restaurant favorite that is topped with Parmesan cheese—a Paleo Diet no-no. The simple addition of garlic and tempting virgin olive oil will keep you from missing the cheese. SERVES 4

4 tablespoons extra virgin olive oil
½ sweet onion, thinly sliced
4 garlic cloves, finely chopped
1 teaspoon dried tarragon
1 teaspoon dried oregano
1 cup broccoli florets
1 cup cauliflower florets
1 cup diced baby carrots
Lemon wedges, to taste
Freshly ground pepper, to taste

Heat olive oil in a cast iron skillet over medium flame. Add onion, garlic, tarragon, and oregano and sauté while stirring for two to three minutes. Add broccoli, cauliflower, and carrots and continue cooking for three to four minutes.

Once the veggies begin to stick to the pan, stir and continue cooking until slightly charred. Turn off heat and cover; let sit for five minutes.

Squeeze lemon wedges over veggies, drizzling juice evenly. Sprinkle with freshly ground pepper.

Asian Slaw

Everyone loves fresh coleslaw in the summer. With the addition of Omega 3 Mayonnaise and a bit of ginger, you can enjoy a healthy version of this picnic side dish. Make it the day before you plan on serving to allow the lemon juice to tenderize the cabbage. SERVES 4

½ head red cabbage, washed and shredded
1 large carrot, peeled and grated
1 teaspoon grated fresh ginger
Juice from ½ lemon
2 scallions, chopped
½ cup Omega 3 Mayonnaise (page 196)
¼ cup diced dried pineapple
1 teaspoon white sesame seeds
1 teaspoon black sesame seeds

Combine the cabbage and carrots in a large flat bowl. Add ginger, lemon juice, scallions, and mayonnaise. Toss thoroughly. Stir in pineapple pieces. Sprinkle with sesame seeds.

Cover and refrigerate for twenty-four hours, remixing every few hours. Remove from refrigerator five to ten minutes before serving.

Cream of Broccoli Soup

Roasting the broccoli and the onion allows the flavors to mellow and combine to produce a wealth of flavor. This is further accented by the rich flavor of roasted walnuts. SERVES 4

2 tablespoons extra virgin olive oil

1 medium yellow onion, diced

2 cups broccoli florets

1 cup Chicken Broth (page 193)

1 teaspoon freshly squeezed lemon juice

1 tablespoon lemon zest

4 tablespoons roasted walnuts

Preheat oven to broil. Heat oil in a cast iron skillet over medium flame. Add onion and sauté for five to eight minutes, until translucent. Add broccoli and stir until well coated.

Place skillet in oven and broil for ten minutes, stirring once. Remove from oven, cover, and let sit for two minutes. Combine broccoli and onion mixture with broth and lemon juice. Puree in a blender until smooth.

Pour soup into serving bowls and garnish with lemon zest and walnuts.

Brussels Sprouts with Shallots and Pecans

Brussels sprouts are high in fiber, vitamin A, potassium, and calcium. Their delicate leaves balance perfectly with the crunch of pecan and the slightly sweet essence of shallot. SERVES 4

8 ounces raw Brussels sprouts
1 ounce raw pecans, chopped
1 tablespoon extra virgin olive oil
2 small shallots, minced
1 tablespoon walnut oil

Remove stem ends of sprouts and cut a crisscross in the bottom of each to ensure even cooking. Fill a 2-quart saucepan with 1 quart of water and bring to a boil. Insert steamer basket, add sprouts, and steam for ten to twelve minutes. Plunge sprouts into a bowl filled with ice water to stop the cooking process. Peel the outer leaves from each sprout and set aside. Chop sprouts and combine with pecans.

Heat olive oil in a cast iron skillet over medium flame, adding the chopped sprouts and pecan mixture. Cook and stir for five minutes. Add shallots and stir an additional minute. Just before serving, add the sprout leaves and cook for one minute. Toss thoroughly with walnut oil.

Caramelized Broccoli with Orange Zest

For a sweet twist on this vitamin-packed veggie, we toss broccoli with orange juice, resulting in a lovely caramelized dish. SERVES 4

2–3 broccoli heads, cut into bite-sized pieces
2 tablespoons extra virgin olive oil
1 teaspoon freshly ground black pepper
1 tablespoon freshly squeezed orange juice
1 tablespoon orange zest
1 tablespoon walnut oil

Preheat oven to broil. Place broccoli in large bowl and toss with olive oil and pepper. Drizzle with orange juice and orange zest and mix thoroughly. Arrange broccoli pieces evenly spaced on a rimmed baking sheet.

Broil for ten to twelve minutes, until bright green and slightly tender. Remove from oven and toss with walnut oil.

Sandy Point Spinach Sauté

Preparing spinach with a quick sauté enhances its flavor while maintaining its superlative nutritional benefits. Spinach is a great source of iron, and you can quadruple its absorption by combining it with a food high in vitamin C, like red bell peppers. SERVES 4

2 bunches spinach
2 tablespoons extra virgin olive oil
4 garlic cloves, diced

1 tablespoon fresh basil, minced
1 tablespoon minced fresh cilantro
1 small red bell pepper, sliced into matchsticks
1 lemon, cut in half

Wash and drain spinach using a salad spinner.

Heat oil in a cast iron skillet over medium flame. Stir in garlic for one minute. Toss in the spinach, basil, and cilantro and mix thoroughly for two minutes. Remove from heat. Top with pepper slices.

Squeeze half of the lemon over the greens and slice the remaining half to use as a garnish.

Dandelion Greens with a Bite

Dandelion greens enhance the flavor of many dishes, particularly when combined with complementary herbs and spices. A bit of juice from a freshly squeezed lime and some red chili pepper flakes add even more zing to this tangy vegetable.
SERVES 4

2 tablespoons extra virgin olive oil
1 small yellow onion, chopped
1 bunch dandelion greens, coarsely chopped
½ lime, cut into wedges
1 teaspoon red chili pepper flakes

Heat oil in a cast iron skillet over medium flame. Add onion, cover, and cook until soft. Add greens and stir, allowing them to cook for two minutes.

Just before serving, drizzle with lime juice on top and sprinkle with chili pepper flakes.

Carb Lover's Cauliflower

If you're missing your mashed potatoes, here's a flavorful but simple idea to use in lieu of that high-glycemic starchy vegetable. The addition of squash helps to thicken this dish without the use of processed starches. Served with a rare filet mignon and a fresh salad, this dish will surely satisfy the meat-and-potato lovers at your table. SERVES 4

> 2 cups cauliflower florets
> 1 large zucchini, sliced into 1-inch rounds
> 2 tablespoons extra virgin olive oil
> 6 garlic cloves, diced
> ½ cup Chicken Broth (page 193)
> 2 tablespoons minced fresh chives
> Freshly ground black pepper, to taste

Fill a 2-quart pot with 1 inch of water and insert steamer basket. Bring water to a boil. Add cauliflower and steam until tender, about ten minutes. Remove cauliflower and set aside to cool. Add zucchini rounds to pot and steam until soft, about ten minutes.

Heat oil in a cast iron skillet over medium flame. Add garlic and cook while stirring for five minutes. Turn off flame and cover. Drain zucchini and let cool for five minutes.

When both cauliflower and zucchini are cool, place in blender and add broth. Add garlic and oil mixture. Puree until smooth. Spoon entire mixture back into pot and heat over low flame, stirring occasionally. Sprinkle with chives and pepper to taste.

Smoky Southern-Style Collards

For anyone who is an aficionado of Southern cooking, it might be surprising to find a reference to this cuisine in keeping with the Paleo Diet. Traditional recipes include hog jowls or feet. In lieu of fatty pork cuts, diced lean turkey sautéed with garlic and onions, and then charred, imparts a savory, smoky flavor to this dish without the saturated fat. SERVES 4

2 tablespoons extra virgin olive oil

1 medium yellow onion, diced

4 garlic cloves, minced

½ teaspoon dried thyme

½ teaspoon dried basil

4 ounces Roasted Turkey Breast, diced (page 90)

2 bunches collard greens, coarsely chopped, with stems removed

Heat olive oil in a cast iron skillet over medium flame. Stir in onion and sauté for five to eight minutes, until translucent. Add garlic and continue stirring for two to three minutes.

Increase heat to high and stir for one minute, lightly charring the onions and garlic. Stir in thyme and basil, reducing flame to medium. Add turkey and cook for two minutes.

Toss in collard greens and cook while stirring for two minutes, making sure to mix all ingredients well.

Eggplant and Basil Sauté

Eggplant recipes often call for large amounts of salt and/or oil, because eggplant acts as a sponge, soaking up almost all the oil you give it. However, with just a little olive oil and a slower cooking time, eggplant has enough time to sweat, which results in a salt-free, tender dish. Nell's inspiration for this dish was a Chinese fast-food take-out option from a place in New York City's Chinatown. SERVES 4

2 tablespoons extra virgin olive oil

2 garlic cloves, minced

1 large eggplant, cut into ½-inch slices after stems have been removed

4 large fresh basil leaves, coarsely chopped

2 tablespoons dried oregano

Heat oil and garlic in a cast iron skillet over medium flame and stir for one minute. Add eggplant slices. Cover and turn every five minutes for twenty minutes. (The eggplant may stick slightly at first; just keep cooking and turning.)

Sprinkle with basil and oregano, cover, and continue cooking for five minutes. Remove from heat and let stand for five minutes before serving.

Braised Leeks with Garlic

Leeks, a member of the onion family, are mild and sweet. Cooking them slowly in liquid develops their subtle flavor. The addition of shallot, white wine, and a hint of garlic turns this dish into the perfect accompaniment for a Paleo main course.

SERVES 4

2 tablespoons extra virgin olive oil
1 medium shallot, diced
2 garlic cloves, minced
2 large leeks, roots and top green portions removed
½ cup dry white wine or Chicken Broth (page 193)
Freshly ground black pepper, to taste

Preheat oven to 200 degrees.

Heat olive oil and shallot in a covered cast iron skillet over medium flame for one minute. Stir in garlic and continue cooking for one minute. Move the garlic and shallot to the sides of the pan to make room for the leeks in the center. Cut leek stems in half lengthwise and place in pan cut side down. Cover and cook for two minutes, turning once.

Remove from heat and turn leeks cut side up. Spread shallot and garlic evenly on top of leeks. Add wine or chicken broth to pan. Cover with foil, place in oven, and steam for forty-five minutes. Leeks are done when tender and fragrant. Remove from oven and cool for five minutes. Cut leeks in half widthwise before serving. Sprinkle with freshly ground pepper.

Flax-Dusted Leafy Greens

Although this recipe calls for chard and/or kale, don't hesitate to try all sorts of leafy green vegetables: spinach, mustard greens, dandelion greens, or beet greens. The greater the variety, the better. SERVES 4

2 bunches rainbow chard or kale, or any combination
   of greens
2 tablespoons extra virgin olive oil
2 tablespoons freshly ground flaxseed

Remove stems from greens and finely chop. Set aside. Coarsely chop the leaves and set aside.

Heat oil in a cast iron skillet over medium flame. Add chopped stems and sauté for two to three minutes. Turn off heat and cover.

Before serving, turn the flame to medium, and add leaves, stirring for one to two minutes. Sprinkle with ground flaxseed.

Wild Roasted Mushrooms

Most mushrooms are prepared with copious amounts of butter or margarine. Our recipe represents a foolproof Paleo-style approach to this flavorful dish. SERVES 4

4 tablespoons extra virgin olive oil
2 garlic cloves, diced
8 ounces cremini mushrooms, coarsely chopped
8 ounces oyster mushrooms, coarsely chopped

3.5 ounces enoki mushrooms, coarsely chopped

1 tablespoon dried basil

1 teaspoon dried tarragon

1 teaspoon paprika

2 tablespoons chopped fresh parsley

Preheat oven to broil. Combine olive oil and garlic in a baking dish. Add mushrooms and sprinkle with basil, tarragon, paprika, and parsley.

Broil for thirty minutes, stirring mixture at the halfway point. Remove from oven and cool for five minutes.

Monterey Mushrooms

The inspiration for this simple dish comes from Nell's local Italian eatery, where it is offered as a compliment of the chef to enjoy while you peruse the menu. Allow this dish an hour or two in the refrigerator to infuse the flavors. Simple but quite tasty. SERVES 4

8 ounces white button mushrooms, sliced

2 tablespoons extra virgin olive oil

2 teaspoons dried oregano

1 tablespoon freshly squeezed lemon juice

Freshly ground black pepper, to taste

Place mushrooms in a large bowl. Combine olive oil, oregano, and lemon juice in a small jar and shake well. Pour over mushrooms and mix until well coated.

Refrigerate and let sit for an hour or two. Add fresh pepper.

Eggplant à la Française
(Ratatouille)

French cooking Paleo style is quick, simple, and delicious. This veggie dish takes only minutes to prepare, which makes it an ideal recipe for the busy cook. *Bon appetit.* SERVES 4

4 tablespoons extra virgin olive oil
1 medium yellow onion, chopped
2 garlic cloves, minced
2 large zucchini, cut into 2 × ½ inch strips
1 green bell pepper, cut into 2 × ½ inch strips
1 yellow bell pepper, cut into 2 × ½ inch strips
1 medium eggplant, cut into 2 × ½ inch strips
2 plum tomatoes, seeded and chopped
1 bay leaf
Fresh parsley, to taste

Heat 2 tablespoons of the olive oil in a cast iron skillet over medium flame. Add chopped onion and sauté for five minutes. Toss in garlic and continue to sauté for one minute. Place zucchini in skillet, stirring occasionally for five minutes. Pour into a bowl and set aside.

Add another tablespoon of the olive oil and bell peppers to skillet. Sauté for five minutes, stirring occasionally. Remove from skillet and set aside. Brush the last tablespoon of olive oil evenly over eggplant and place in skillet. Cook for five minutes, stirring occasionally. Place zucchini and peppers back in skillet with the eggplant. Mix in tomato, bay leaf, and parsley. Cover and cook for ten minutes. May be served warm or cold.

Raving Rapini

This cousin to broccoli brings a delectable twist to the Paleo table. For those who are learning to enjoy new veggies and want something familiar in the mix, raisins offer a bit of sweet to balance the taste. SERVES 4

1 bunch rapini (broccoli rabe)
1 lemon
1 teaspoon dried dill
1 teaspoon basil
2 tablespoons cold-pressed flaxseed oil
¼ cup sun-dried tomatoes
2 tablespoons raisins

Coarsely chop rapini and place in a cast iron skillet with 1 inch water. Steam for about five minutes until bright green, stirring once or twice to ensure even cooking. Drain and cool for five minutes. Squeeze half of the lemon into a small jar. Add dill, basil, and flaxseed oil. Cover and shake. Toss into rapini, then add sun-dried tomatoes and raisins. Cut the other half of the lemon into wedges for a garnish.

Roasty Toasty Beets with Hazelnuts

Fresh beets are very tasty. Roasting this root vegetable brings out its flavor, which is further enhanced by the delectable hazelnut finish. SERVES 4

1 bunch beets, leaves removed and beets quartered
2 tablespoons extra virgin olive oil
1 tablespoon dried basil
1 garlic clove, pressed
2 tablespoons chopped roasted hazelnuts (filberts)
Freshly ground black pepper, to taste

Preheat oven to broil. Toss beets with olive oil, basil, and garlic in a glass or ceramic baking dish.

Broil for thirty minutes, stirring once at the halfway point. Top with roasted hazelnuts and pepper.

Nell's Original Raw Kale Fusion

This dish is best prepared the day before serving to allow the kale to marinate and soften. SERVES 4

1 head red kale, coarsely chopped, with stems removed
1 head green kale, coarsely chopped, with stems removed
½ small red onion
2 garlic cloves
2 tablespoons extra virgin olive oil
2 tablespoons cold-pressed flaxseed oil
Juice from 1 lime
Freshly ground black pepper, to taste
1 fresh heirloom or beefsteak tomato
2 orange slices

Place kale in a wide shallow bowl.

Combine red onion and garlic in a small food processor and pulse until finely chopped. Add garlic and onion mixture to kale. Toss in oils and lime juice and mix thoroughly. Sprinkle with freshly ground pepper.

Cover with plastic wrap and refrigerate; stir two or three times over the next twenty-four hours. Just before serving, chop the tomato and add it to the kale mixture. Garnish with orange slices.

Back-to-Our-Roots Winter Veggies

Roasted root veggies are a delicious, Paleo-friendly winter dish, with hearty and savory flavors to warm up cold winter nights. Leftovers can be tossed in the blender and turned into delicious hot soups. SERVES 4

2 medium turnips, peeled and cut into ½-inch pieces

2 medium parsnips, peeled and cut into ½-inch pieces

1 medium rutabaga, peeled and cut into ½-inch pieces

1 medium yam, cut into ½-inch pieces

1 medium yellow onion, chopped

2 tablespoons extra virgin olive oil

1 whole garlic bulb

1 sprig fresh rosemary, stem removed

Freshly ground black pepper, to taste

Preheat oven to 400 degrees. Spread turnips, parsnips, rutabaga, yam, and onion evenly on a large rimmed baking sheet and drizzle with oil. Wrap garlic bulb in foil and place in middle of baking sheet.

Scatter rosemary leaves over the veggies. Bake for one hour and stir occasionally to ensure even cooking. Remove from oven.

Remove foil from garlic and place in center of serving dish. Arrange veggies around the garlic. Sprinkle with freshly ground black pepper. Garlic can be easily pressed from skin for a tasty addition.

Baked Holiday Stuffing

When the holidays roll around, you will be able to enjoy special foods with just a few substitutions and the addition of healthy ingredients. This Paleo recipe is a truly fantastic alternative to traditional stuffing. Enjoy and celebrate! SERVES 4

2 tablespoons extra virgin olive oil
4 large celery stalks, diced
1 medium yellow onion, diced
4 portobello mushrooms, coarsely chopped
1 medium shallot, minced
½ cup Chicken Broth (page 193)
2 tablespoons freshly ground flaxseed
2 tablespoons minced fresh sage
4 ounces Brazil nuts, toasted and coarsely chopped

Preheat oven to 350 degrees.

Heat olive oil in a cast iron skillet over medium flame. Add celery, onions, and mushrooms and stir occasionally for ten minutes. Toss in shallot and continue cooking for two minutes. Pour in broth and stir. Remove from heat.

Stir in flaxseed, sage, and Brazil nuts. Bake for twenty minutes.

Tokyo Sesame Wakame

As sashimi fans know, seaweed is the perfect side dish to pair with this Japanese delicacy. Unlike most restaurant versions, this Paleo recipe is healthy and delicious. SERVES 4

2 ounces wakame (purchase a brand that is entirely
   seaweed with no additives)
2 tablespoons cold-pressed flaxseed oil
2 large carrots, grated
2 scallions, finely chopped
1 tablespoon freshly squeezed lemon juice
½ teaspoon black sesame seeds
½ teaspoon white sesame seeds

Put the dried seaweed in 2 cups of water and let sit for ten minutes, then drain. Add the flaxseed oil, carrots, scallions, and lemon juice. Toss and sprinkle with black and white sesame seeds.

11

Condiments, Salad Dressings, Sauces, and Fruit Purees

One of the gifts brought to you by *The Paleo Diet Cookbook* is the return of your palate as Mother Nature always intended it to be. Real food will slowly and surely become more enticing to your tastes as artificial foods laced with unnatural combinations of fat, carbohydrates, salt, and sugar are left by the wayside. Give it some time—a few weeks or more—and you will begin to taste the subtleties of fresh fruits, vegetables, herbs, pungent seafood, and rich, grass-fed meats. Sugary pastries, ice cream, and chocolate will suddenly begin to taste too sweet. Spaghetti, pasta, bread, cereals, french fries, and potato chips will become starchy gut bombs that make you feel bloated and awful. As you lose weight, become fit, and reach your genetic potential, you will crave real food, not the starchy, sugary processed products that have made Americans the fattest people on earth.

Listen to your body. Once you have cleaned out the salt, the sugars, the refined oils, and the processed foods from your former diet, they will no longer taste as good as you remember them, and if you are like most people, upon reintroduction these foods will make you feel uncomfortable and bloated.

Condiments, salad dressings, and sauces play a crucial role in modern-day Paleo Diets because they add flavor, texture, and visual appeal to almost any dish. The key here is to make your own condiments that aren't filled with refined sugar or salt, or high in omega 6 vegetable oils or other additives. Paleo condiments, salad dressings, and sauces add luxury, subtle flavors, and overtones to the cornucopia of real unadulterated foods that are the basis of modern Paleo eating.

Creamy Coconut Curry

This Paleo-friendly recipe produces a wonderful blend of sweet and spicy flavors, making it a great pairing for meat and fish dishes. MAKES 1 CUP

2 tablespoons extra virgin olive oil

1 medium onion, chopped

1 small tomato, chopped

4 garlic cloves, crushed

1 1-inch piece fresh ginger root

1 teaspoon salt-free garam masala spice blend

8 ounces fresh, whole coconut milk

Heat oil in a cast iron skillet over medium flame. Add onion and tomato. Cook for five minutes. Stir in ginger and garlic and continue cooking for one minute. Reduce heat to low and simmer for ten minutes while stirring occasionally. Add garam masala and continue to simmer for five minutes. Remove from heat and cool for ten minutes.

Pour into a blender and puree until smooth. Return mixture to skillet and add coconut milk. Simmer over low heat, stirring constantly for ten minutes. Serve warm or cold.

Apricot Chutney

This recipe creates a sweet mixture that pairs quite well with red meat, pork, and lamb. Top off your favorite Paleo meats with this proven crowd pleaser. MAKES 1 CUP

4 medium apricots, coarsely chopped
1 teaspoon freshly grated ginger
1 teaspoon ground cardamom
1 tablespoon raisins
1 tablespoon chopped roasted cashews

Combine apricots with ginger and cardamom in a food processor on low setting. Ingredients should be mixed rather than pureed.

Place in a serving bowl and add raisins. Mix well. Sprinkle with roasted cashews.

Classic Marinara Sauce

A perfect accompaniment to spaghetti squash, Paleo marinara sauce is fast and easy to prepare. Like soups and stews, this sauce is tastier the next day, after all the flavors have had a chance to mingle. MAKES 2 CUPS

2 tablespoons extra virgin olive oil
1 medium yellow onion, chopped
2 garlic cloves, diced
4 medium tomatoes, chopped
¼ cup red wine
1 tablespoon minced fresh oregano

1 tablespoon minced fresh basil
1 bay leaf

Heat olive oil in a cast iron skillet over medium flame. Add onion and sauté for five minutes. Mix in garlic and cook for one minute. Stir in tomatoes and wine and continue cooking for five minutes.

Add oregano, basil, and bay leaf. Cover and reduce heat to low. Simmer for twenty minutes.

Walnut, Flaxseed, and Avocado Dip

This delicious dip is flavorful and packed with omega 3 to keep your mind and body sharp. Try it with your favorite fresh veggies or as a spread for a Paleo wrap. MAKES ½ CUP

½ cup raw walnuts
1 tablespoon flaxseed oil
1 tablespoon walnut oil
1 tablespoon finely chopped fresh cilantro
1 tablespoon freshly squeezed lemon juice
1 tablespoon freshly squeezed lime juice
½ medium avocado, pit reserved
1 tablespoon freshly ground flaxseed (flax meal)

Combine walnuts, flaxseed oil, walnut oil, cilantro, and lemon and lime juices in a food processor. Puree until smooth. Add avocado and puree until well blended.

Transfer mixture from food processor to serving bowl. Stir in flax meal. Place avocado pit in the center to delay browning.

Tangy Tomato Salsa

Because of its versatility, salsa is one of our favorite ways to liven up any Paleo dish. If you prefer your salsa on the chunky side, leave the food processor behind and mix it up in a bowl. Either way, you'll love this flavorful treat. MAKES 1 CUP

2 tablespoons freshly squeezed lime juice
2 tablespoons diced red onion
2 tablespoons minced fresh cilantro
1 garlic clove, minced
2 medium tomatoes, diced
1 teaspoon red chili pepper flakes

Combine lime juice, red onion, cilantro, and garlic in a food processor. Process until well blended.

Add the tomatoes and red chili pepper flakes and puree for two minutes. Chill for one hour before serving.

Peach Salsa with a Punch

This fresh summertime recipe offers a twist on a classic favorite. The sweetness of the peach contrasts nicely with the zing of the onion and the pop of the red chili pepper flakes. This salsa works equally well as a dip for fresh veggies or a topping for grilled fish. MAKES 1 CUP

2 fresh peaches, washed and coarsely chopped
1 tablespoon freshly squeezed lime juice

2 tablespoons diced red onion

1 tablespoon minced fresh cilantro

1–2 teaspoons red chili pepper flakes

Place peaches in medium bowl. Add lime juice and stir. Toss in onion and cilantro.

Combine with 1 teaspoon red chili pepper flakes; if a spicier taste is desired, add 1 additional teaspoon. Refrigerate for one hour before serving.

Paleo Pesto

Here is a sauce or a dip that will make any vegetable or protein more exciting. While different regions of Italy have their own traditional pesto recipes, the one common thread is often the inclusion of Parmesan or Asiago cheese. We've mixed it up to make this recipe Paleo perfect. MAKES ½ CUP

1 cup loosely packed basil leaves, stems removed
   and discarded

2 tablespoons extra virgin olive oil

1 tablespoon flaxseed oil

1 tablespoon walnut oil

1 tablespoon freshly squeezed lemon juice

2 garlic cloves

Freshly ground black pepper, to taste.

Combine basil leaves, oils, lemon juice, and garlic in a food processor. Blend until thoroughly combined. Add freshly ground black pepper.

Holy Guacamole

This universal favorite is a must for any Paleo dieter's repertoire. Guacamole goes well on top of omelets, salads, or soups or as a delicious veggie dip. Save the avocado pit to place in the middle of the dip as a preventive measure against browning. MAKES 2 CUPS

2 whole avocados
¼ cup chopped tomato
2 tablespoons chopped fresh cilantro
2 tablespoons minced red onion
1 tablespoon freshly squeezed lime juice
Cayenne pepper

Cut avocados in half and remove pits. Scoop out avocado flesh and place in medium bowl. Mash well with a fork until all large chunks are broken up. Add tomato, cilantro, onion, and lime juice. Mix well.

Transfer mixture to a serving bowl and place avocado pit in the center. Dust with cayenne pepper to taste.

Holiday Cranberry Sauce

Who doesn't enjoy a side of cranberry sauce to celebrate the holidays? This Paleo version will satisfy your festive appetite with all the benefits that this seasonal fruit has to offer. MAKES 1½ CUPS

8 ounces fresh, whole cranberries

1 tablespoon orange zest

2 tablespoons freshly squeezed orange juice

1 tablespoon toasted, slivered almonds
(optional)

Combine cranberries with 1 cup of water in a saucepan. Bring to a boil. Reduce heat to medium and continue cooking until cranberries start to pop. Cover pot to prevent splattering and continue cooking, for a total of fifteen minutes.

Remove from heat and stir in orange zest, orange juice, and almonds. Cool for thirty minutes. Refrigerate for at least one hour before serving.

Salad Dressing Starter

Use this starter recipe to create a variety of flavorful dressings. Let your personal taste preferences be your guide when adding herbs and spices for your signature Paleo dressing.

MAKES ½ CUP

5 tablespoons plus 1 teaspoon avocado, walnut, flaxseed, or olive oil

2 tablespoons plus 2 teaspoons freshly squeezed lemon, lime, or orange juice

Freshly ground black pepper, to taste.

Combine all ingredients in a food processor and blend thoroughly. Use as is, or add herbs and spices as desired.

Essential Aioli

Traditional aioli calls for garlic, olive oil, and raw egg. While eating a raw egg can be done safely, preparing this basic sauce without it is easier, risk-free, and delicious. Serve as a topping for steamed veggies, as a base for soups, or as a marinade for meat. MAKES ½ CUP

4 large garlic bulbs
4 teaspoons extra virgin olive oil

Preheat oven to 400 degrees. Remove the outer layer of garlic skin from the bulbs. Cut off the very top of each bulb and discard. Place bulbs on a 6 × 6–inch piece of aluminum foil. Lift each corner of the foil to create a basket shape. Drizzle 1 teaspoon olive oil on each bulb. Fold the edges together, sealing the basket.

Cook for forty-five minutes. Remove from oven, discard foil, and let cool for five minutes. Using your fingers, press garlic cloves to extract pulp. Discard skins. Place pulp in food processor and puree until smooth.

Chicken Broth

Chicken broth is easy enough to find in a grocery store, but making your own is simple and efficient and guarantees that you're getting pure Paleo. MAKES 2 QUARTS

1 stewing chicken, 4–5 pounds
2 celery stalks, chopped
2 large carrots, chopped
1 small yellow onion, chopped
1 bay leaf

Place chicken in a 3-quart stockpot with enough water to cover. Add celery, carrots, onion, and bay leaf. Heat on stove over high flame and bring to a boil. Reduce heat to low.

Cover pot and simmer for two to three hours, stirring occasionally. Remove from heat and skim off the foam that has risen to the top of the water.

Drain broth through a colander and into a large container. When chicken is cool enough to handle, remove meat from bones and use in your favorite Paleo recipe or as a simple snack. Broth may be used in sauces, stews, soups, or frozen for future use.

Baba Ghanoush

Do you miss hummus as a dip for fresh veggies? Here's an alternative that you can enjoy without having to stray from the realm of Paleo living. The garlic and the eggplant can be broiled at the same time. Just be sure to keep track of the difference in cooking times. MAKES 2 CUPS

1 small garlic bulb
3 tablespoons extra virgin olive oil
1 large eggplant
½ teaspoon freshly squeezed lemon juice

Preheat oven to broil. Place garlic bulb in the center of a 4 × 4–inch piece of foil. Drizzle with 1 tablespoon of the oil. Fold edges over top of bulb to create a seal.

Place in oven and broil for forty minutes. Cut off top and bottom of eggplant and discard. Slice eggplant lengthwise into four equal pieces. Brush both sides of the pieces with the remaining 2 tablespoons of olive oil. Place in oven on wire rack next to garlic. Broil for thirty-two minutes and turn every eight minutes. Eggplant flesh should be soft and browned.

Remove eggplant from oven and let sit until cool enough to handle. Remove garlic from oven and set aside. When cool, remove skin from eggplant and discard. Place flesh in a food processor. Press garlic from bulb, discarding skin. Add garlic pulp to food processor. Puree briefly until smooth. Add lemon juice and puree again for fifteen seconds. Place in serving bowl and serve warm or cold.

Pineapple-Peach Puree

Whipping fruit into a puree is an easy, tasty way to create a snack that can be eaten as is, mixed with protein powder for a preworkout snack, or topped with roasted nuts for a light dessert. Mix and match your favorite fruits for an endless variety. SERVES 4

½ small pineapple, rind removed and cut into chunks
2 medium peaches, peeled and coarsely chopped

Place both fruits in a food processor and puree until smooth.

Pumpkin Puree

This recipe calls for only one ingredient and can be used to create smoothies or as an addition to soups. The trick is in knowing how to prepare the pumpkin before it is pureed. SERVES 2 OR 3

1 small pumpkin

Preheat oven to 400 degrees. Cut pumpkin in half and remove seeds. Place in baking dish cut side down and add 1 inch of water. Bake for forty-five minutes. Pumpkin is done when skin is easily pierced with a fork.

Remove from oven and let cool. Scoop out flesh and place in food processor. Puree until smooth.

Strawberry-Banana Puree

This famous twosome is always a hit. Choosing a banana that's not too ripe is the trick to keeping this variation from being too starchy and sweet. SERVES 4

2 bananas, ripe but not spotty
1 cup hulled strawberries

Combine fruits in a food processor and puree until smooth. Chill for thirty minutes.

SOME ORIGINAL PALEO DIET FAVORITES

These much-loved condiment, sauce, and salad dressing recipes from my first book, along with their brand-new counterparts in this chapter, can become delicious flavor-enhancing treats as you become more acquainted with Paleo cuisine. You may not think of mayonnaise, catsup, vegetable dip, or tartar sauce as very Paleo, but these time-tested scrumptious versions of the originals are indeed pure Paleo. Such beloved condiments and dressings will help you make the transition to the Paleo Diet and may serve as a starting point to create your own savory Paleo recipes and meals.

Omega 3 Mayonnaise

MAKES 1 CUP

1 egg
1 tablespoon freshly squeezed lemon juice
¼ teaspoon dry mustard
½ cup olive oil
½ cup flaxseed oil

Put egg, lemon juice, and mustard in a blender and blend for three to five seconds. Continue blending as you slowly add oils.

Blend until the mayonnaise is thick. Scrape mayonnaise into a snap-lock plastic container and refrigerate. The mayonnaise should keep for five to seven days.

Veggie Dip

MAKES 1 CUP

1 cup Omega 3 Mayonnaise (see recipe above)
1 teaspoon dried dill
½ teaspoon garlic powder
Freshly ground black pepper, to taste

Mix all ingredients together. It is better if refrigerated for one hour before serving, but this step is not necessary. Makes a great dip for raw veggies or for use as a salad dressing.

Tartar Sauce

MAKES 1¼ CUPS

1 cup Omega 3 Mayonnaise (see recipe above)
¼ cup finely chopped red onion
1 tablespoon freshly squeezed lemon juice
½ teaspoon dried dill
¼ teaspoon paprika
Pinch of garlic powder

Mix all ingredients together. Chill prior to serving.

Ray's Catsup

MAKES ABOUT 2 CUPS

3½ pounds tomatoes, sliced

2 medium onions, sliced

1 very small garlic clove

½ bay leaf

½ red bell pepper

¼ cup unsweetened fruit juice (white grape, pear, or apple)

1 teaspoon whole allspice

1 teaspoon whole cloves

1 teaspoon whole mace

1 teaspoon celery seeds

1 teaspoon black peppercorns

1 ½-inch cinnamon stick

½ cup freshly squeezed lemon juice

Pinch of cayenne pepper

Boil tomatoes, onions, garlic, bay leaf, and red pepper until soft. Add fruit juice. Mix allspice, cloves, mace, celery seeds, peppercorns, and cinnamon in a small cloth spice bag and add to mixture. Bring to a boil quickly, stirring frequently until the mixture reduces to half the quantity. Remove spice bag. Add lemon juice and cayenne pepper. Continue boiling for ten minutes more.

Bottle catsup in clean jars, leaving ¾ inch of space at the top of each jar for expansion. Seal and freeze immediately. Always refrigerate the container that is currently in use.

Source: Ray Audette, *Neanderthin: A Caveman's Guide to Nutrition* (New York: St. Martin's Press, 1999).

Spinach Salad Dressing

MAKES 5 CUPS

3 tablespoons dry mustard

1 garlic clove, minced

1 tablespoon freshly ground black pepper

1 teaspoon cayenne pepper

1 teaspoon paprika

1 cup Burgundy wine

1 cup pureed fresh tomatoes

2 cups flaxseed oil

1 cup freshly squeezed lemon juice

Combine all ingredients in a blender. Pour into a cruet and shake well before each use.

Omega 3 Russian Salad Dressing

MAKES 1½ CUPS

1 cup fresh tomatoes

½ cup flaxseed oil

½ cup freshly squeezed lemon juice

3 tablespoons freshly squeezed orange juice

1 teaspoon paprika

1 small scallion, coarsely chopped, or 1 teaspoon
    onion powder

1 teaspoon horseradish powder (optional)

1 garlic clove (optional)

Put all ingredients in a blender and blend until smooth.

Omega 3 Tomato Dressing

MAKES 1½ CUPS

⅓ cup fresh tomatoes
½ cup flaxseed oil
⅓ cup lemon juice
1 garlic clove
1 onion, chopped

Put all ingredients into a blender and blend until smooth.

Raspberry Barbecue Sauce

MAKES ABOUT 1½ CUPS

2 teaspoons olive oil
¼ cup minced onion
1 tablespoon minced jalapeño pepper
¼ cup Ray's Catsup (page 198)
1 tablespoon honey
¼ teaspoon dry mustard
¼ teaspoon cayenne pepper
2 cups fresh or frozen raspberries

Heat oil in a cast iron skillet and sauté onion and jalapeño pepper for about ten minutes. Add catsup, honey, mustard, and cayenne and heat until mixture simmers. Add raspberries and simmer for an additional ten minutes.

Remove from heat and let cool. Pour into a blender and blend until smooth.

12

Paleo Beverages and Desserts

I f we followed in the footsteps of our Stone Age ancestors, Paleo beverages would be pretty boring—that is, unless you want to drink nothing but water for the rest of your life. Fortunately for us, we have the technical means to produce beverages that are not only healthy but also pleasing to our palates. Smoothies, particularly if mixed with a protein such as egg white, are wholesome, restore muscle glycogen, and promote muscle building. Freshly juiced fruits and veggies yield a nutritious beverage rich in vitamins, minerals, and photochemicals.

However, if you are overweight or have metabolic syndrome symptoms (high blood pressure, abnormal blood lipids, type 2 diabetes, or heart disease), restrict or eliminate all fruit and vegetable juices. For those in good health, remember the 85-15 rule, which allows you a glass of wine or two with your dinner. When in doubt about beverages, drink water.

The ground rules for modern-day Paleo desserts are simple: no refined sugars, grains, or honey. Focus on fresh fruits, dried fruits, nuts, spices, herbs, fruit purees, and even veggies. For instance, shredded carrots make a great topping for a bowl of cubed apples and raisins. Paleo desserts should share the style of the rest of the meal: they should be simple, nutritious, visually appealing, and appetizing, like virtually all of the recipes we have presented in this book. Paleo desserts may be served anytime and don't necessarily need to be included at the end of a meal. We enjoy nibbling on fresh succulent grapes right along with our main course.

If desserts are to balance the rest of the meal, they need distinct flavors and personalities of their own. Spices and extracts that can enhance fresh fruits include almond extract, allspice, anise, caraway seeds, cardamom, cinnamon, cloves, ginger, lemon extract, mace, mint, nutmeg, orange extract, rum extract, and vanilla extract. Draw on your imagination but be cautious, as excessive use of spices and extracts may leave a muddled flavor in your dessert. Ideally, a fruit dessert should emphasize only a few spices and flavors. For example, fresh strawberries cut lengthwise taste heavenly with cinnamon and vanilla extract. Some of the stronger and earthier Paleo dessert flavors include anise, clove, cinnamon, and walnuts.

Desserts should be cooling to the palate. Sorbets and tropical fruit flavors are perfect, but the ingredients are not available year-round. In wintertime, hearty and comforting desserts such as rhubarb, baked apples, or nut-stuffed dates may appeal to you. On a chilly night, they will satisfy your sweet tooth without sacrificing your health.

Sticky, sugary-sweet desserts may give your taste buds a temporary blitz, but they eventually will let you down as your blood sugar level plummets. In contrast, Paleo desserts will leave you satisfied but not full. You will sleep soundly and wake up rested and ready for your next Paleo meal, knowing that your dessert was as good for your body as it was for your palate.

Powered-Up Smoothies

For Paleo Dieters, a smoothie is a nutritious and delicious meal that is quick and easy to prepare. Endurance athletes find this easily digestible, energy-packed drink a great preworkout option. The use of brewed herbal tea offers the added benefit of antioxidants without sacrificing taste. Double the recipe to serve two, or take the second serving with you for a mid-day snack.

SMOOTHIE STARTER

Begin your smoothie with this nutritious base, followed by one of our vitamin-packed additions. Use your imagination and personal favorites to make your own fabulous creations. Many Paleo Dieters find this the perfect way to rise and shine each day.

> 8 ounces brewed, chilled herbal tea of your choice
> 1 scoop plain egg white protein powder
> 1 tablespoon freshly ground flaxseed
> 1 tablespoon almond or walnut butter
> ½ cup crushed ice

Puree all ingredients in a blender on high speed for two minutes. Use as a base and add the ingredients from any of the following recipes. Blend well and enjoy!

BANANA BLAST

      1 large banana

      ½ teaspoon nutmeg

COCOBERRY DREAM

      1 tablespoon coconut oil

      ½ cup fresh or frozen blueberries

      ½ cup hulled fresh strawberries

      ½ cup fresh blackberries

MELON MANIA

      ½ cup cubed fresh honeydew melon

      ½ cup cubed fresh cantaloupe

      ½ teaspoon cinnamon

PEACHY KEEN

      ½ cup fresh peaches and/or nectarines

      ½ cup apricots

      1 teaspoon cinnamon

      1 teaspoon nutmeg

LUAU AT SUNRISE

      1 cup cubed fresh pineapple

      ½ cup fresh orange slices

      1 banana

      1 tablespoon coconut oil

PUMPKIN PLEASER

Use fresh brewed, chilled, black tea in your Smoothie Starter for this holiday favorite.

      ¾ cup Pumpkin Puree (page 195)

      ¼ teaspoon nutmeg

      ¼ teaspoon cinnamon

Paleo Piña Colada

This kid-friendly version of the tropical classic goes perfectly with fajitas and guacamole. SERVES 2

1 cup water
1 tablespoon unrefined coconut oil at room temperature
1 cup fresh coconut milk
12 ounces frozen pineapple cubes
Pineapple wedges

Combine water, coconut oil, and coconut milk in a blender. Puree until smooth. Add pineapple cubes and puree until thoroughly combined.

Pour into chilled glasses and garnish with pineapple wedges.

Mango Margarita Mambo

This is a refreshing choice on a hot summer day. Skip the ultra-sweet, corn-syrupy taste of a premade mix and use this light and healthy option instead. Our friends at CrossFit occasionally liven this concoction up with a shot or two of good tequila. SERVES 2

1 cup water
1 cup frozen mango cubes
2 tablespoons freshly squeezed lime juice
Lime wedges

Combine water and mango cubes in blender and puree until smooth. Add lime juice and puree again. Pour into chilled glasses. Garnish with lime wedges.

Spa Water

This recipe is inspired by health spas, where a variety of fruit-infused waters is served. Try it with "flat" water in lieu of sparkling to make it even more creative. SERVES 2

2 cups natural sparkling mineral water
½ orange, sliced into rounds
½ lemon, sliced into rounds
1 small kiwi, sliced into rounds
4 mint leaves

Combine water with fruit slices in a glass pitcher. Shred two mint leaves and mix with water and fruit. Place in refrigerator one hour before serving.

Pour into glasses and garnish with remaining mint leaves.

Baked Apples

Missing that old-fashioned apple pie? The craving stops here. Enjoy the sweetness of this traditional Thanksgiving treat, while the mouthwatering aromas fill your kitchen. You won't miss the heavy, gluteny crust and the butter. SERVES 4

2 tablespoons raisins

2 tablespoons chopped raw walnuts

1 teaspoon ground cinnamon

4 small Golden Delicious, Pippin, or Granny Smith apples, peeled and cored

Preheat oven to 375 degrees. Combine raisins, walnuts, and cinnamon in a small bowl and mix thoroughly.

Evenly divide the raisin mixture into four portions and stuff into hollows of apples. Place upright in glass or ceramic baking dish and add 1 inch of water. Bake for thirty to forty minutes. Apples are done when soft and easily pierced with a fork. Cool for five minutes before serving.

Spiced Apples

Reinvent this recipe each time it's made by choosing different types of apples. Opt for Granny Smith if something tart is desired or a Golden Delicious for something on the sweet and mellow side. Adding a splash of lemon juice to the sliced apples will prevent browning. SERVES 4

2 large apples of any variety, cored and sliced
2 tablespoons freshly squeezed lemon juice
¼ teaspoon clove powder
¼ teaspoon ground ginger
¼ teaspoon ground allspice
½ teaspoon ground cinnamon

Place apple slices in a medium bowl. Combine remaining ingredients in a small jar and pour over apple slices. Toss gently to ensure even coating.

Lorraine's Strawberries with Crème

Summertime in our neck of the woods means the strawberries are fresh and ripe for picking. For generations, this sweet fruit has been served laden with heavy sugars and creams. This tradition is now being kept alive with a Paleo version to honor the desserts made for us by our great-grandmothers.
SERVES 4

2 cups sliced strawberries
½ teaspoon vanilla extract
½ cup fresh full-fat coconut milk

Place a copper bowl and a whisk in the freezer to chill for thirty minutes. Place strawberries in a medium bowl and add vanilla. Stir gently to mix. Cover and refrigerate for thirty minutes.

Pour coconut milk into copper bowl and whisk until mixture thickens slightly. Place berries in small bowls and top with coconut crème.

Pat's Peach Granita Almondine

Lorrie's mother, Pat, prepared fresh peach dishes throughout the months of summer. She would have enjoyed this Paleo recipe, with all the flavorful ingredients to enhance the sweet tastes of this popular stone fruit. SERVES 4

3 large peaches, peeled, pitted, and coarsely chopped
½ teaspoon real almond extract
¼ teaspoon ground nutmeg
¼ teaspoon ground ginger
2 tablespoons slivered almonds, toasted

Place peaches, almond extract, nutmeg, and ginger in a food processor and puree until smooth.

Pour into a glass baking dish, cover with foil, and place in freezer for three hours. Every thirty minutes, use a fork to scrape and loosen the puree. Top with slivered almonds.

Cherry-Berry Medley

Berry lovers will find this recipe to be the perfect satisfying ending to a Paleo meal. The unusual pairing of fruits makes for a surprisingly delicious combination. SERVES 4

½ cup Bing or Rainier cherries, pitted and chopped
½ cup blueberries

½ cup golden raspberries

½ cup blackberries

1 teaspoon vanilla extract

½ teaspoon clove powder

½ teaspoon ground cinnamon

1 tablespoon chopped fresh mint leaves, plus 4 leaves for garnish

Combine cherries and berries in a medium bowl. Add vanilla, clove, cinnamon, and chopped mint and gently toss. Chill for thirty minutes. Garnish with mint leaves just before serving.

Rook's Tropical Paleo Pottage

Sweet and simple, this dish takes only minutes to create and goes well paired with any Paleo meal. This vitamin- and potassium-loaded dessert will keep you healthy while satisfying your sweet tooth. SERVES 4

1 large yam, cubed

2 large plantains, cubed

¼ cup freshly squeezed orange juice

4 tablespoons natural flaked coconut

Preheat oven to 400 degrees. Combine yam and plantain in rectangular baking dish. Pour in orange juice. Scatter with coconut. Cover and bake for thirty minutes.

Marjorie's Kona Grillers

Hawaiians know that the pineapple is the most abundant and versatile of the fruits found on the islands. Try this delicious grilled version with your favorite pork or poultry dish. The enhanced sweetness brought out by the grilling will surprise you. SERVES 4

2 tablespoons extra virgin olive oil
1 teaspoon freshly squeezed lime juice
¼ teaspoon ground cardamom
¼ teaspoon ground coriander
¼ teaspoon ground cinnamon
½ small pineapple, cut into 1-inch wedges

Turn grill to medium flame or preheat oven to broil. Combine oil, lime juice, and spices in a small jar and shake well. Brush over pineapple wedges to coat thoroughly. Grill or broil for twenty minutes, turning at halfway point.

Brandied Fruit Compote

We can't resist the bold flavor of this sweet dessert. Top off your meal with this flavorful infusion of fruits, spices, and nuts and enjoy the abundance of nutritional benefits to keep you healthy. SERVES 4

2 large pears, peeled and sliced
2 small plums, halved
2 tablespoons brandy
½ teaspoon ground allspice
¼ teaspoon clove powder
4 tablespoons chopped walnuts

Preheat oven to 400 degrees. Combine pears and plums in a medium bowl. Mix together brandy, allspice, and clove. Pour over fruit and gently toss.

Divide into four ramekins. Cover and bake for twenty minutes. Change oven setting to broil. Scatter walnuts over fruit and brown for three minutes.

Banana Bonanza

Surprising is the only way to describe this dessert. The ordinary banana quickly transforms itself when combined with these delicious ingredients. Enjoy with your family and friends for a potassium-packed flavor bonanza. SERVES 4

2 large, very ripe (spotty) bananas
1 teaspoon pure vanilla extract
¼ teaspoon ground ginger
¼ teaspoon ground allspice
4 tablespoons pecans, toasted and finely chopped
Freshly ground nutmeg, to taste

Cut bananas in half lengthwise. In a small jar, combine vanilla, ginger, and allspice and shake well. Brush over bananas.

Place bananas cut-side down on wax paper. Freeze for thirty minutes. Top each banana with 1 tablespoon of the pecans and season with nutmeg to taste.

13

The Paleo Diet
Two-Week Meal Plan

I n this chapter, we have created a two-week meal plan to help you take the guesswork out of getting started. For Paleo veterans, it may give you some new ideas and twists for making the Paleo Diet even more delicious and user-friendly. For the newbies, what better way to make the transition to the Paleo Diet than by having a road map to guide you along your way?

The preparation time for most meals is twenty minutes or less, and for many, less than ten minutes. Follow these simple but delectable daily menus, and you will immediately notice positive changes in your energy level, mental outlook, and sleep patterns. After two weeks, you will be well on your way to becoming a dedicated Paleo Dieter. *Bon appetit*!

The recipes marked with an asterisk can be found in this book.

Sunday

BREAKFAST	Wild Salmon Delight* ½ grapefruit Herbal tea
SNACK	Lean beef slices 2 apricots
LUNCH	Paleo Tilapia Tacos* Mixed Herb Salad* Spa Water*
SNACK	Apple slices ¼ cup raw walnuts
DINNER	Cream of Broccoli Soup* Coconut-Cashew Chicken* Tomato and cucumber slices Pat's Peach Granita Almondine* 1 glass white wine or mineral water

Monday

BREAKFAST	Banana Blast Smoothie* Hard-boiled eggs
SNACK	Apple with ¼ cup raw walnuts
LUNCH	Grilled salmon on a bed of spinach with mandarin orange slices and slivered almonds Herbal tea
SNACK	Sliced lean beef (flank steak) ½ cup melon balls

DINNER	Chicken Braised with Celery*
	Mixed green salad, topped with blueberries and olive oil
	Kiwi slices
	Mineral water

Tuesday

BREAKFAST	So Cal Omelet*
	½ grapefruit
	Herbal tea

| SNACK | Steamed broccoli drizzled with olive oil and topped with shredded chicken (use last night's leftovers) |

LUNCH	Lean turkey breast on mâche, drizzled with flaxseed oil and lemon
	Fresh pear slices
	Spa Water*

| SNACK | Mixed fresh berries |
| | 2 chopped hard-boiled eggs |

DINNER	Paleo Tuna Niçoise*
	1 cup red or green grapes
	Baked Apples*
	Herbal tea

Wednesday

BREAKFAST	Shrimp Scramble*
	Fresh mixed blueberries and raspberries
	Herbal tea

SNACK	Cucumber, carrot, and apple, chopped and tossed in olive oil, lemon juice, and mint leaves
LUNCH	Cactus Salad* Sliced mango Herbal tea
SNACK	2 Tropical Deviled Eggs*
DINNER	Caramelized Broccoli with Orange Zest* Bison-Stuffed Bell Peppers* Signature Salad* ½ cup sliced strawberries 1 glass red wine or mineral water

Thursday

BREAKFAST	Turkey Gobbler's Omelet* Tangerine segments Herbal tea
SNACK	Apple with ¼ cup raw almonds
LUNCH	Mixed green salad with Salad Dressing Starter* Sliced lean beef, topped with blueberries Steamed artichoke Herbal tea
SNACK	Sliced bell peppers ½ avocado, sliced and drizzled with lime and cilantro
DINNER	Greek Salata à la Paleo* Ike's Moussaka*

Marjorie's Kona Grillers*
Mango Margarita Mambo*
1 glass white wine or mineral water

Friday

BREAKFAST Roast turkey breast drizzled with olive oil
            and basil
            Sliced apples
            Herbal tea

SNACK   Steamed broccoli sprinkled with freshly
            ground flaxseed
            Navel orange

LUNCH   Strawberry-Spinach Salad*
            Carne Asada*
            ½ cup raspberries
            Spa Water*

SNACK   Pear slices
            ¼ cup raw pecans

DINNER   Cedar-Plank Salmon*
            Sandy Point Spinach Sauté*
            Tossed green salad
            Iced herbal tea

Saturday

BREAKFAST Melon Mania Smoothie*
            Poached eggs

SNACK   Shredded kale, tossed with lime juice, olive
            oil, and minced red onion and topped with
            chopped turkey breast

LUNCH	Salmon Caesar Salad* (use leftover salmon from last night)
	Sliced tomatoes
	½ cup fresh pineapple chunks
	Herbal tea

| SNACK | Grapes |
| | ¼ cup raw walnuts |

DINNER	Spaghetti Squash Italiano*
	Paleo Chicken Saltimbocca*
	½ cup sliced peaches
	French Country Salad*
	Paleo Piña Colada*

Sunday

BREAKFAST	Eggciting Veggie Frittata*
	Spiced Apples*
	Herbal tea

| SNACK | Sliced honeydew melon |
| | Sliced turkey breast |

LUNCH	Grilled Chicken Salad* (use leftover chicken from last night)
	½ cup fresh blackberries
	Spa Water*

| SNACK | Chili-Lime Shrimp* |

DINNER	Beef Tenderloin Roast*
	Mikey's Mâche Salad*
	Carb Lover's Cauliflower*
	½ cup watermelon chunks
	1 glass red wine or mineral water

Monday

BREAKFAST   Spicy Breakfast Burrito*
             Steamed broccoli
             Herbal tea

SNACK   ½ cup blackberries and raspberries mixed
               with slivered almonds and tossed with
               fresh basil

LUNCH   Glenrock Steak Salad*
             1 fresh peach, sliced
             Spa Water*

SNACK   Melon Blankets*

DINNER   Asparagus Starter*
             Sweet and Savory Swordfish*
             Arugula-Avocado Salad*
             Sunchoke Sauté*
             ½ fresh pomegranate, or seasonal fruit
             Spa Water*

Tuesday

BREAKFAST   Fired-Up Steak and Eggs*
             Fresh cucumber spears
             Water with fresh lemon

SNACK   Veggie Virtuoso*

LUNCH   Cactus Salad*
             Sliced mango
             Herbal tea

SNACK   Asian pear
             Raw walnuts

DINNER	Grapes of Wrap*
	Arugula Avocado Salad*
	Paleo Fajita Stir-Fry*
	Steamed asparagus spears
	1 glass red wine or mineral water

Wednesday

| BREAKFAST | Morning Rainbow* |
| | Herbal tea |

| SNACK | 1 fresh orange |
| | 2 sticks Paleo Warrior's Jerky* |

LUNCH	Leftover Paleo Fajita Stir-Fry*
	½ cup cantaloupe cubes
	Tossed green salad
	Herbal tea

SNACK	Steamed zucchini, chopped and tossed with
	flaxseed oil and lemon juice
	Grilled chicken breast

DINNER	Grilled Snapper*
	Nutty Beet Salad*
	Watermelon slices
	Steamed veggies
	Herbal tea

Thursday

BREAKFAST	Fired-Up Steak and Eggs*
	Fresh seasonal fruit
	Herbal tea

SNACK	1 fresh apple
	¼ cup Spicy Mixed Nuts*
LUNCH	Sliced turkey breast
	Spinach with sliced strawberries, drizzled
	with flaxseed oil
	Papaya spears
	Spa Water*
SNACK	2 Tropical Deviled Eggs*
DINNER	Gazpacho*
	Asian Slaw*
	Paleo Spicy Tuna Rolls*
	Grapefruit wedges
	Mineral water with fresh lime

Friday

BREAKFAST	Morning Rainbow*
	Melon slices
	Mineral water with fresh lemon
SNACK	Beefed-Up Mini Wraps*
LUNCH	Paleo Tamales in Banana Leaves*
	Steamed asparagus
	Orange slices
	Spa Water*
SNACK	Peach slices
	10 raw macadamia nuts
DINNER	Pecan-Stuffed Figs*
	Perfect Pot Roast*
	Flax-Dusted Leafy Greens*

Fresh seasonal fruit
1 glass red wine or mineral water

Saturday

BREAKFAST   Cocoberry Dream Smoothie*
2 poached eggs
Herbal tea

SNACK   Veggie Virtuoso*

LUNCH   Perfect Pot Roast* (use last night's leftovers)
Mixed green salad with avocado slices
Cherry-Berry Medley*
Herbal tea

SNACK   Sliced carrots and bell peppers, dipped in
Holy Guacamole*

DINNER   Roasted Trussed Chicken*
Blasted Veggie Medley*
Greek Salata à la Paleo*
Lorraine's Strawberries with Crème*
1 glass white wine or mineral water

14

Treats and Meals for CrossFitters and Athletes

Anytime a new book, popular song, movie, or scientific discovery is recognized on the world's stage, the process has as much to do with the people who embrace the thought, creation, or idea as with the person or people who created it. Accordingly, I extend my gratitude and appreciation to all CrossFitters and athletes worldwide who have embraced the Paleo Diet as their nutritional plan for achieving maximal performance and optimal health and well-being. Your support and enthusiasm for humankind's native diet has made "Paleo" a household word. Thank you!

For athletes and very active people, a few necessary tweaks are required to the Paleo Diet to help you maximize performance. Although Joe Friel and I have written extensively about these slight adjustments in my second book, *The Paleo Diet for Athletes*, I'll emphasize some of the key points you need to keep in mind as you prepare your meals and snacks.

The basic rules of the game—lean meats, seafood, fresh fruits and veggies, nuts, and healthy oils—still apply. However, to fuel your muscles for long runs, swims, bicycle rides, and other hard workouts, you will need to eat concentrated carbohydrate sources to refuel muscle glycogen, particularly before and after workouts. Yams, sweet potatoes, bananas, dried fruit, fruit juices, very high sugar and high sugar fresh fruits (see chapter 1) are great sources of concentrated starches and sugars. Unlike refined grains, they are net alkaline-yielding, thereby preventing the loss of the amino acid glutamine from your bloodstream, which helps to preserve your muscle mass.

In the post-exercise period, besides consuming concentrated sugars and starches, make sure that you get plenty of lean protein. This is your best source of the three branched-chain amino acids (leucine, isoleucine, and valine) that directly stimulate muscle growth and regeneration. Listed on page 227 are the total branched-chain amino acid concentrations in 1,000-calorie servings of common foods.

Food	Total Branched-Chain Amino Acids (Grams)
Dried egg white (84% protein)	43.4
Raw egg white	43.0
Whey protein (80% protein)	35.4
Lean meat	33.6
Soy protein (70% protein)	32.9
Hard-boiled egg	13.3
Milk	12.1
Beans	11.9
Fresh vegetables	7.7
Whole grains	6.1
Nuts and seeds	4.6
Starchy root vegetables	1.7
Fruits	0.8

Obviously, I don't recommend concentrated whey or soy proteins, milk, beans, or whole grains as sources of branched-chain amino acids, because these are non-Paleo foods that adversely affect your health and well-being. If you don't have an allergy to eggs or an autoimmune disease, egg whites added to fresh fruit smoothies make ideal post-exercise drinks. These delicious drinks are concentrated sources of branched-chain amino acids, and the easily digestible, blended fruits rapidly restore your muscle glycogen. Check out Chris's Famous Post-Ride Smoothie (page 231). It's delicious as well as good for you.

Notice that small amounts of salt are included in a number of recipes in this chapter. Adding small quantities of salt to your meals and snacks is perfectly acceptable for hardworking athletes, who may lose excessive salt in their sweat.

A final note: I don't recommend potatoes for anyone, athletes included, because they are not only high-glycemic-load foods but also concentrated sources of two saponins (alpha chaconine and alpha solanine) that compromise the intestinal barrier.

Baked Paleo Yam "Fries"

For Paleo endurance athletes, the choices offered by marketed sports nutrition products leave a lot to be desired. Yams are an excellent alternative to help fuel the body for training and racing, and the addition of a pinch of salt helps to prepare for the electrolytes that will be lost through sweat. Easy, tasty, and without the saponins found in potato-derived french fries, these tasty treats will store quite well in the refrigerator and are a perfect choice for right before or after your endurance workout. SERVES 4

2 large yams
2 tablespoons extra virgin olive oil
1 tablespoon garlic powder
Salt and black pepper to taste
Cayenne pepper, to taste (optional)

Preheat oven to broil. Slice yams lengthwise into ½-inch strips. Toss with oil and garlic powder, coating evenly. Place on a rimmed baking sheet lined with parchment paper. Broil for twenty minutes and turn at the halfway point. Yams are done when easily pierced with a fork.

Remove from oven and sprinkle with salt and pepper to taste. Add cayenne pepper to taste. Cool for five minutes.

Athlete's Cinnamon Applesauce

Easy to digest and quick to eat, this snack is the perfect choice before a quick speed session at the track or a workout at the pool. Nell likes to pair applesauce with hard-boiled eggs before her training sessions. SERVES 4

> 2 cinnamon sticks
> 4 large Golden Delicious apples, peeled, cored, and chopped
> 1 teaspoon vanilla extract

Fill a 4-quart stockpot with 1 inch of water and insert a steamer basket. Place cinnamon sticks in basket and bring water to a boil. Add apples and cook for twenty minutes, until soft. Cool for five minutes and place in a food processor. Puree until smooth. Stir in vanilla and chill for thirty minutes before serving.

Christina's Espresso-Soaked Figs

A bit of caffeine before endurance workouts paves the way for a slight boost during your training session. The quick release of sugar from the figs serves as a last-minute topping-off for your glycogen stores. Make extra and refrigerate to have on hand for your next session. SERVES 2

> 4 dried figs
> 4 ounces espresso, freshly brewed

Soak figs in espresso for a few minutes.

Post-Workout Banana-Coconut Whip

A great option for a post, short-session workout, this tasty treat is quick and easy to prepare. Enjoy post-workout to restore your potassium levels and refuel your tank. SERVES 2

2 large, very ripe (spotty) bananas
1 scoop egg white protein powder
4 teaspoons natural flaked coconut
Freshly ground nutmeg, to taste

Puree bananas in a food processor until smooth. Add half of the egg white powder and puree, then add the remaining powder. Puree all ingredients until well blended. Top with coconut and nutmeg to taste.

Long Haulers

Many of the sports nutrition products available to athletes are little more than candy bars in disguise. This nifty snack is a great option to bring along on that century ride or an epic hike. SERVES 4

2 large yams, baked
4 tablespoons almonds, slivered and toasted
1 teaspoon ground cinnamon
1 teaspoon kosher salt

Cut yams in half lengthwise. Divide almonds into four equal portions and press into the flesh side of each yam. Sprinkle with cinnamon and salt. Cover with plastic and shape into a roll. Place in freezer for thirty minutes.

Chris's Famous Post-Ride Smoothie

An essential part of an endurance athlete's repertoire is the recovery drink. Replenishing glycogen stores, rebuilding your muscles, and restoring your energy are important after any workout. This delicious smoothie does it all, with fresh fruit ingredients that can be changed every time to keep it interesting.

8 ounces brewed black tea, chilled and unsweetened
½ cup crushed ice
1 scoop plain egg white protein powder
2 bananas
1 scoop L-glutamine powder
Pinch of salt

Combine tea and ice in a blender and whip for one minute. Add protein powder, bananas, L-glutamine, and salt. Puree until blended. Serves one.

SUGGESTED VARIATIONS

BANANA-MELON: banana with watermelon juice

TROPICAL DREAM: mango with pineapple juice

POTASSIUM PUNCH: cantaloupe with orange juice

APPLE ORCHARD BREEZE: pear with apple juice

Unraisinably Delish Spiced
Yam Puree

Another great option for pre- or post-workout, this holiday snack can be enjoyed any time of year. SERVES 2

2 large yams, baked
1 teaspoon kosher salt
¼ teaspoon ground nutmeg
¼ teaspoon ground cinnamon
¼ teaspoon freshly ground allspice
4 tablespoons raisins

Place yams in a food processor and puree until smooth. Stir in salt, nutmeg, cinnamon, and allspice. Top with raisins.

"Fill 'er Up" Endurance Breakfast

Start your workout with a full tank of premium fuel in your system. Easily digestible foods with a higher glycemic load than that of your normal, day-to-day meals will help you to reach all of your training goals. SERVES 2

> 2 Banana Blast smoothies (page 205)
> 1 large baked yam
> Pinch of salt

Prepare smoothies. Cut yam in half lengthwise and sprinkle with salt.

Afternoon Top-Off

Trying to keep on top of your glycogen stores for that second workout of the day? Eating real food in place of a prepackaged product will keep you on top of your game. SERVES 1

> 1 banana
> 4 egg whites
> Ground nutmeg, to taste
> Pinch of salt

Slice banana into 1-inch pieces and combine with egg whites in a small bowl. Sprinkle with nutmeg and salt. Should be eaten one hour before working out.

Grueler Chicken

A balanced way to fuel up your tank for the next day's long, grueling workout sessions, this meal is not for the chicken-hearted. Packed with all the Paleo ingredients you'll need for a great training session, this chicken-yam recipe will quickly become a favorite. Serve it with our Blasted Veggie Medley (page 164) as a side dish. SERVES 4

2 Roasted Trussed Chicken breasts (page 82)
2 tablespoons extra virgin olive oil
2 large baked yams, halved lengthwise
Freshly ground black pepper

Slice each chicken breast in half. Heat oil in a cast iron skillet over medium flame. Place cooked chicken in skillet to reheat.

Add yams, flesh side down, and cover. Heat for five minutes, turning at halfway point. Season with pepper to taste.

Rebound Power Breakfast

Eating a meal high in protein after a killer strength workout will allow you to reap the greatest benefit from all your hard work.

SERVES 2

2 teaspoons extra virgin olive oil

8 omega 3 eggs

1 small tomato, diced

2 scallions, diced

1 teaspoon dried basil

4 ounces Roasted Turkey Breast, diced (page 90)

Cayenne pepper, to taste

Heat oil in a cast iron skillet over medium flame. Beat eggs in a small bowl with a wire whisk. Pour into skillet and cook for two minutes, lifting up edges with a plastic spatula every thirty seconds.

Add tomato, scallions, basil, and cooked turkey. Fold over, cover, and cook for two minutes. Cut in half and slide onto two plates. Season with pepper to taste.

Race-Night Celebration

After a hard race or competition, you'll likely be ready for a hearty meal. It's time to enjoy this celebratory meal that will replenish your energy and help your body to recover for the next big event. Serve the following bison burgers with our Baked Paleo Yam "Fries" (page 228) and Sandy Point Spinach Sauté (page 168). SERVES 2

1 pound lean ground bison
2 tablespoons extra virgin olive oil
2 large butter or Bibb lettuce leaves
½ avocado, sliced
¼ small red onion, sliced
Paleo condiments of your choice (see chapter 11)

Ignite the grill to medium flame. Combine bison with oil and shape into two large patties. Grill for fifteen minutes, turning at the halfway point. Place in lettuce leaves and top with avocado, onion, and condiments.

RESOURCES

Recommended Web Sites

Loren Cordain's Paleo Diet Web site
www.thepaleodiet.com

Loren Cordain's Dietary Cure for Acne Web site
http://www.dietaryacnecure.com/

Robb Wolf's Web site
http://robbwolf.com/

Don Wiss's comprehensive Paleo Web site
http://paleodiet.com/

Recommended Books

Cordain, Loren. *The Dietary Cure for Acne*. Fort Collins, CO: Paleo Diet Enterprises LLC, 2006.

———. *The Paleo Diet, Revised Edition: Lose Weight and Get Healthy by Eating the Foods You Were Designed to Eat*. Hoboken, NJ: John Wiley & Sons, 2011.

Cordain, Loren, and Joe Friel. *The Paleo Diet for Athletes: A Nutritional Formula for Peak Athletic Performance*. Emmaus, PA: Rodale Press, 2005.

Suppliers of Paleo-Related Foods

Paleo Brands
http://www.paleobrands.com/

Suppliers of Game Meats

Broken Arrow Ranch
3296 Junction Highway
Ingram, TX 78025
(800) 962-4263
www.brokenarrowranch.com

Exotic Meat Market
130 Walnut Avenue, Unit A-18
Parris, CA 92571
951-345-4623
http://exoticmeatmarket.com/

Exotic Meats USA
1330 Capita Blvd.
Reno, NV 89502
(800) 444-5687
www.exoticmeatsandmore.com/

Game Sales International
P.O. Box 7719
Loveland, CO 80537
(800) 729-2090
www.gamesalesintl.com

Grand Natural Meat
P.O. Box 10
Del Norte, CO 81132
(888) 338-4581
www.elkusa.com

Hills Foods Ltd.
Unit 130 Glacier Street
Coquitlam, British Columbia
Canada V3K 5Z6
(604) 472-1500
www.hillsfoods.com

Mount Royal Game Meat
3902 N. Main
Houston, TX 77009
(800) 730-3337
www.mountroyal.com

Polarica
105 Quint Street
San Francisco, CA 94124
(800) 426-3872
www.polarica.com

Suppliers of Pasture- and Grass-Produced Meats, Eggs, and Dairy

Jo Robinson's comprehensive listing of pasture and grass-fed meats, eggs, and dairy in the United States and Canada
http://www.eatwild.com/

INDEX

fruits (*continued*)
    in Chris's Famous Post-Ride Smoothie, 231
    Christina's Espresso-Soaked Figs, 229
    Coconut-Cashew Chicken, 82
    coconut foods, 36–37
    Creamy Coconut Curry, 185
    Elk Tenderloin in Cherry Reduction, 119
    ground rules for, 16–19
    Holiday Cranberry Sauce, 190–191
    juices, 28
    Melon Blankets, 72
    Paleo Piña Colada, 206
    Peach and Ginger Scallops, 131
    Peach Salsa with a Punch, 188–189
    Post-Workout Banana-Coconut Whip, 230
    Powered-Up Smoothies, 204–205
    Raspberry Barbecue Sauce, 200
    Salmon Fillet with Nectarine Infusion, 140
    Shrimp and Pineapple Skewers, 140–141
    Spa Water, 207
    Strawberry-Banana Puree, 196
    Strawberry-Spinach Salad, 154–155
    See also athletes, recipes for; desserts; fruit
      purees; *individual meat dishes*

game meat
    Elk Tenderloin in Cherry Reduction, 119
    Ground Duck Burgers with Rosemary, 93
    Herbed Roasted Pheasant, 94
    lean choices for, 14
    Ostrich Almondine, 120
    Pan-Seared Duck Breast, 92
gardening, 51
Gazpacho, 70
Glenrock Steak Salad, 155
gliadin, 30
glycemic load, 16, 31
glycoalkaloids, 31
grains, 10, 11–12, 26, 30–32, 35
Grapes of Wraps, 71
grass-fed meats, 112–113
Greek Chicken Breast Kebabs, 83
Greek Salata à la Paleo, 152
Grilled Chicken Salad, 152–153
Grilled Snapper, 132
Ground Duck Burgers with Rosemary, 93
Grueler Chicken, 234

Hatano Research Institute (Japan), 23

heart disease, 127
Herbed Roasted Pheasant, 94
Holiday Cranberry Sauce, 190–191
Holy Guacamole, 190
Homewood Chicken, 81

Ike's Moussaka, 109–110
insulin, 31, 96–97

jerky, 111–113
    do-it-yourself foods, 50
    Paleo Warrior's Jerky, 121
Julienned Veggie Stir-Fry, 160

kitchen guidelines, 33–34
    budgeting for Paleo diet, 49–51
    checklist for non-Paleo foods, 38–41
    cooking temperature, 47–48
    kitchen tools, 45–47
    leftover foods, 52
    organic foods, 51–52
    purging non-Paleo foods, 34–38
    restocking kitchen with Paleo supplies,
      41–45
    sanitation, 48–49
knife sets, 46

lamb, 95–97
    Ike's Moussaka, 109–110
    lean choices for, 14
lauric acid, 36–37
"leaky gut," 30–32
lectins, 31
leftover foods, 52
legumes, 10, 20, 26–27
locally grown food, 50
Long Haulers, 230
Lorraine's Strawberries with Crème, 209

macadamia oil, 23
Mango Margarita Mambo, 206
Mango-Strawberry Olé, 68–69
Marjorie's Kona Grillers, 212
meats, 10–11
    fat and protein content in, 12
    fatty, 27
    feedlot and grain-produced meats, 11–12
    lean choices for, 13–14
    processed, 12–13, 38